IN THE VINEYARD OF THE LORD

IN THE VINEYARD
OF THE LORD

---

*The Life, Faith, and
Teachings of Joseph Ratzinger
Pope Benedict XVI*

Marco Bardazzi

Rizzoli

PHOTO CREDITS: 1. EPA/Erzbistum/Landov, 2. EPA/Erzbistum/Landov, 3. EPA/Erzbistum/Landov, 4. MAXPPP/KNA Landov, 5. EPA/Erzbistum/Landov, 6. MAXPPP/KNA/Landov, 7. dpa/Landov, 8. KNA/SIPA, 9. MAXPPP/KNA/Landov, 10. dpa/Landov, 11. © 2005 Karsten DE RIESE (AGENTUR FOCUS/CONTACT PRESS IMAGES), 12. MAXPPP/KNA/Landov, 13. REUTERS/Kai Pfaffenbach/Landov, 14. REUTERS/Osservatore Romano-Arturo Mari/Pool/Landov, 15. EPA/Landov, 16. EPA/Landov

For the texts by His Holiness John Paul II, His Holiness Benedict XVI, and the Congregation for the Doctrine of the Faith © Libreria Editrice Vaticana

First published in the United States of America in 2005 by
Rizzoli International Publications, Inc.
300 Park Avenue South
New York, NY 10010
www.rizzoliusa.com

© 2005 Marco Bardazzi

Translated from the Italian by Michael F. Moore

2005 2006 2007 2008 / 10 9 8 7 6 5 4 3 2 1

ISBN: 0-8478-2801-8

LIBRARY OF CONGRESS CONTROL NUMBER: 2005926979

Printed and bound in the United States

CONTENTS

1. ROMAN SPRING

Wojtyla's Ruse

A solitary man, his white hair covered by a beret, walked at a brisk pace through the twilight of a spring evening in Rome. Lost in silent thoughts, in silent prayers, he passed the two great colonnades of Saint Peter's Square, designed by Gian Lorenzo Bernini, which wrapped in their embrace all the Christians in the world. Through Saint Anne's gates he continued his walk to the Vatican to visit his dying friend. The pope, who more than twenty-six years before first looked out on the Square and opened his arms to the festive crowd like Bernini's colonnade, was near death.

Few passersby on that spring evening recognized Cardinal Joseph Ratzinger. Those who did silently made the sign of the cross.

Ratzinger walked toward the pope's apartment in the Apostolic Palace, where his friend Karol Wojtyla, John Paul II, had lived for more than a quarter of a century in three simple rooms with minimal furnishings and no luxuries. There was a nineteenth-century bed with a solid wooden headboard, a crucifix, an old lamp on a wooden side table, and photos of the pope's father, Karol, and his mother, Emilia, on the bedside table. Pope John Paul II lay dying surrounded by these few simple things. Ratzinger lived nearby, in an apartment on the fourth floor of a building just outside the Vatican proper.

In 1981, John Paul II summoned Ratzinger to Rome, taking him away from his native Germany. The cardinal was by the pope's side from that time on. With the passage of the years, he started to think that the time had come to step aside, to go back to his studies in his beloved Bavaria. On various occasions after his seventy-fifth birthday, he attempted to raise the question with John Paul II but the reply was always an affectionate, "Yes, we'll have to talk about this later."

The moment to take his leave from the Vatican never arrived for the seventy-eight-year-old cardinal. Instead, the moment when Ratzinger was going to take his leave from the pope was fast approaching. Among the thoughts that occupied him on that spring evening was perhaps the latent, troubling idea that his friend had created one final ruse to prevent him from leaving Rome.

A few days later, on April 19, 2005—the feast of Saint Leo IX, an eleventh-century Alsatian pope—beneath a gray, overcast sky, the man who until a few days earlier entered and exited the Vatican walls with little fanfare and wearing a simple beret on his head, like a Roman everyman, appeared on the balcony of Saint Peter's. This time a crowd of hundreds of thousands and a worldwide television audience were watching him. This time he had a new name: Benedict XVI. He was the 265th pope in history, the first in the third millennium, and the first German pope to be elected in 950 years, since Victor II in 1055.

"Pope Wojtyla has prevented him from returning to Germany once again," commented the smiling spokesman for the Holy See, Dr. Joaquin Navarro-Valls, at a media briefing soon after.

With the death of his friend, "his" pope, Joseph Ratzinger's days

of walking along the ancient streets of Borgo Pio or across Saint
Peter's Square, dining in his favorite restaurant, Cantina Tirolese,
and visiting the parish on the outskirts of town, Santa Maria Con-
solatrice, are at an end. At an age when most men decide that the
time has come to retire, the former cardinal is making his entrance
into history.

The legacy left to him by John Paul II is much greater than the
nineteenth-century bed in the pope's apartment. In fact, he hesi-
tated to take the place occupied for more than twenty-six years by
a pope whom the people immediately proclaimed a saint.

When the Roman Catholic Church lost its leader on April 2,
some commentators claimed that the death of John Paul II truly
brought the twentieth century to a close. One thing was certain: his
successor would have to bear witness to the two-thousand-year
history that began with the apostle Peter in order to help Catholics
deal with the challenges of the twenty-first century.

The issues facing Benedict XVI at the beginning of his papacy
would be daunting for any man, whether in terms of the vision of
Catholicism internally or in the role of the Church on the world
stage.

A Complex Legacy

The popes of the second half of the last century, especially John
XXIII and Paul VI, began to broaden the horizon of the
Church's activities in the world. But it is with John Paul II that the
Catholic Church became a global player in every sense.

Benedict XVI is now the focal point not only for the over one
billion baptized Catholics in the world, but also for the multitudes
of men and women of other religions—or of no religion—who in

the past years saw John Paul II as an appealing model of humanity, and to whom the pope offered himself as a spokesman for human rights and human dignity.

The new pontiff must come to terms immediately, however, with the reservations that the Catholic world has begun to express in recent decades regarding the teachings of the Holy See, which Cardinal Ratzinger defended as prefect of the Congregation for the Doctrine of the Faith. Sexuality, the family, scientific frontiers, and the role of women in the Church are just some of the controversial areas in which Benedict XVI will have to confront modern thinking and popular opinion, as he did for years in his capacity as a cardinal.

The younger generations, many of whom may have acclaimed John Paul II, have difficulty accepting the Vatican's stance on issues such as contraception, although there are signs of growing attention to the idea of abstinence. The use of condoms has been a complex subject for years, especially in Africa and particularly in the context of the fight against AIDS.

Abortion continues to be one of the battlefields on which the Catholic Church expresses itself most forcefully, even when it is at the center of political debate, as it is in the United States. The same is true for euthanasia and for the death penalty. The defense of the sacredness of life, from conception to the last breath, is an issue on which the new pope will have no second thoughts: for the Vatican, interrupting life through human initiative, excluding the Mystery of Life, is, simply put, a mortal risk for humankind. According to Catholic doctrine, it is a question of respect for the dignity of the person, which must be defended against aggressions or discrimination of any type.

The agenda of the pontiff combines old and new challenges in dealing with issues of the family and new models of what family is.

In addition to divorce, to which the Catholic Church has always been opposed, there is the growing phenomenon of civil unions between same-sex partners.

Research laboratories throughout the world carry great promises for humankind, but they also pose new challenges for the papacy. The use of embryos to carry out stem-cell research has long been a source of concern and intense criticism from the Church hierarchy. Cloning, assisted fertility, gene therapy, and the whole area of bioethics will be subjects of debate for years to come. On these and other issues, the Holy Father will make his opinions heard, and forcefully so.

Within the Church itself, Benedict XVI will have to address the crisis in vocations, the difficulties of the missions, and the pressure being applied by many bishops who would like greater collegiality, indicative of the eternal desire of those at the periphery of power to play a larger role in decision making. The role to be assigned to women in the future is another difficult issue destined to come to the fore, not so much in terms of female priests—a concept for which there is no room in Catholicism—but in terms of the possibility of greater participation of women in the management of the Catholic community.

The plague of priest pedophiles, and the full dimensions of the problem that came to light especially in the United States, provides further grounds for reflection and for action in reorganizing the management of the Catholic Church.

Looking Out at the World

The sweeping vista over Saint Peter's Square that Benedict XVI saw from his window is representative of the wide-ranging opportunities for evangelization as well the many challenges he faces. One such challenge is in Europe, where Christianity is diminishing and where the Vatican struggles to make its moral authority felt. At a time when the continent is being changed by a declining birth rate and an increasing immigration rate, especially from Islamic countries, Europe is having an identity crisis in which Christianity is no longer recognized as a common root of European civilization.

On the other side of the Mediterranean, while the 143 million African Catholics are only 13 percent of that continent's population, it is nevertheless the part of the world where Catholicism is growing in the largest numbers, even with risk of more frequent clashes with Islam.[1] Africa, which was so beloved by John Paul II, will continue to be central to the vision of the Holy See, because it is there more than anywhere else that the embodiment of so many of the views embraced by him are found. John Paul II, who helped to bring down communism, was the man who pointed his finger at the excesses and risks of capitalism and who continued to exhort wealthy countries to pay attention to the crises throughout Africa. Poverty, an inequitable distribution of resources, the fight against hunger and epidemics, and questions over the future direction of globalization have serious consequences in Africa; and the Vatican sees the continent as the place where the often empty promises made by the international community should be transformed into action.

In the Middle East, Benedict XVI can continue the dialogue that was started with the Islamic world and at the same time address the need for survival of the Catholic Church in countries where it is in decline. The Vatican is in search of new ways to handle what appears to be a crucial theme of the twenty-first century:

relations between the West and Islamic countries. Contrary to scenarios of a "clash of civilizations," the Catholic Church is looking for innovative ways to reach out to moderate Islam—which represents the majority—and work together to isolate the more radical factions of the Islamic world. The need has become urgent in the wake of the attack on the United States on September 11, 2001, and the new global issues that have come to the fore as a result. Equally delicate are relations with Israel and more generally with Judaism, an area where John Paul II was a true innovator.

In the Middle East and the Gulf, new tensions came into play between the Holy See and Washington after the rejection of war in Iraq uttered by John Paul II—first in 1991 and then in 2003. Future American military initiatives that the Vatican considers unjustified will receive a warning similar to the one issued by him: "War is an adventure without return."[2]

For the most part, Asia, with the exception of the Philippines, is still a frontier and a destination for Catholic missions. Only 10 percent of the continent's inhabitants profess the Catholic faith and certain realities make life very difficult for followers of Catholicism. The most significant case is China, where eight million Catholics still are forced to practice their faith in secret. The pope's unfulfilled dream of a trip to China, like that of visiting Russia and mending relations with the Eastern Orthodox Christians, is now in the hands of his successor.[3]

Moscow is one of the most challenging legacies left behind by John Paul II. Relations with Eastern Orthodoxy continue to be tense—the message from Russia to the Vatican being to "cease the missionary activity" of Catholics. A papal visit in the shadow of the Kremlin still seems far off at the beginning of the pontificate of Benedict XVI.

In North America, the United States is undoubtedly a fertile terrain for the Catholic Church. Aside from the fact that there are sixty-six million Catholics in the country—the numbers have increased in recent decades because of immigration from Latin America—there are undeniable signs of a new dialogue underway within the Christian world between the followers of Rome and Protestants of various denominations. On issues such as bioethics or abortion, common ground has often been found between churches that regarded each other with suspicion in the not-too-distant past. The pedophilia scandal, however, cast a shadow of resentment and suspicion on the priesthood and on the Vatican leadership, creating wounds that will take years to heal.

The most interesting corner of the world for the Catholic Church in the new millennium is Latin America. Almost half of the world's Catholics live somewhere between Mexico and the Tierra del Fuego, in Argentina. Yet while only fifty years ago more than 90 percent of Latin Americans were Catholic, today the figure has dropped to 70 percent.

The great challenge the pope faces here is the huge increase in evangelical Christianity. The Baptists, in particular, are engaged in wide-scale proselytism in South America, and the Catholic Church is struggling to propose an equally attractive model of life and faith.

In Brazil, the country with the largest Catholic population in the world, according to a study by the University of Notre Dame, the figure has gone from 99 percent one century ago to 84 percent in 1995 and 74 percent today. From 1991 to 2000, the number of evangelical Christians grew by 8 percent every year, while the number of Catholics grew only by 0.28 percent. The figures are not much different in other countries. In Argentina, followers of the evangelical churches have grown by 10 percent per year over the past five years. Ninety-eight percent of Peruvians were Catholic in 1940, while today 12 percent of the population belongs to one of the evangelical churches. In 1992, 77 percent of Chileans professed the Catholic faith, but in only ten years the figure has dropped to 71 percent.[4]

Benedict XVI will have to find a way to send more priests to the parishes of Latin America, where Protestant pastors are increasing at a rate that is impossible for the Catholic Church to duplicate, since it takes much longer to prepare its priests in the seminaries. While in today's Europe there is one priest for every 1,385 Catholics and in Asia the ratio is 2,408 to one, in Latin America for every priest there are approximately 6,364 souls in search of assistance.[5]

Christ, the Center of History

However much geopolitical and statistical realities may interest analysts, journalists, and experts, and however clearly they depict the challenges facing this new papacy, in truth they are secondary to the factors that have moved the successors of Peter for more than two thousand years.

To understand the steps that Pope Benedict XVI will take, it is essential to keep in mind that foremost is the desire to render personal witness to "Christ as the center of the cosmos and of history," as John Paul II affirmed in his encyclical *Redemptor hominis*.

Whether taking a position on bioethics or undertaking a visit to a remote part of the world, the pope starts from the idea that Christianity is the true realization of the human spirit. In this perspective, it is inevitable that when he speaks of equality, human dignity, or freedom, he does so according to a judgment of reality that has never been and will never belong to the common outlook.

On April 18, before the beginning of the conclave from which he emerged as pope, Ratzinger already outlined in the homily of that day's mass the terms of the challenge, denouncing what he called "the dictatorship of relativism, which recognizes nothing as absolute and posits as the ultimate measure the ego and its desires."

"To have a clear faith, according to the creed of the Church," he stated, "is often labeled as fundamentalism. While relativism, namely allowing oneself to be buffeted about by the wind of any doctrine whatsoever, appears to be the only attitude in keeping with modern times."[6]

A "clear faith" is something that Joseph Ratzinger has always had, ever since he was a boy, and he has never shied away from defending it.

2. BAVARIA

The Dark Years

In an idyllic setting at the foot of the Alps, in a fairy-tale atmosphere enhanced by Disneyesque castles and reminders of Princess Elizabeth of Bavaria, affectionately known to her subjects as Sissi, this region has since ancient times been a sentimental favorite of Europe. In its forests and along the Inn and Danube rivers, in the green valleys of a piece of the continent hemmed in between Germany, Austria, and the Czech Republic, it has been the scene over the centuries of the rise and fall of the Holy Roman Empire and countless battles between kings, dukes, and various nobles.

Unreceptive to Martin Luther's Reformation, which brought turmoil to German Christianity in the sixteenth century, rural Bavaria has remained at its core a place where a solid, popular Catholicism is still the foundation for community life. The history it shares with neighboring Austria has given rise to a deep central European culture and a great flowering of thought. Yet it is in this area of Europe that one of the great tragedies of modern history also began to take form: nazism.

The last king of Bavaria, Ludwig III, ascended to the throne on the eve of World War I, but he capitulated in 1918 in the wake of peaceful mass protests, led by the socialist Kurt Eisner, culminating in the march on Munich and the bloodless fall of the monarch. Ludwig III fled with his family and shortly thereafter abdicated formally.

Eisner's peaceful revolution quickly disintegrated into violence between the various factions of his movement. The shaky government installed in Munich soon ran into trouble, amid the unrest provoked by clashes between the splintered social democrats, anarchists, and communists. In February 1919, Eisner decided to step down from the government, but he was assassinated before he could formally announce his resignation. The social democrat Johannes Hoffmann, a group of writers, and finally the communists all tried in succession to get the Bavarian government back on its feet, only to see it taken over in the end by the German army.

In March 1920, Gustav von Kahr established a reactionary government in Munich, and various subgroups and minor parties began to form in the shadow world that he created. On January 5, 1919, by the initiative of Anton Drexler, the German Workers' Party was born in the Bavarian capital city. In August 1920 the organization was transformed into the National Socialist Workers' Party (NSDAP), later nicknamed the Nazi party, whose early adherents included an Austrian corporal and failed artist by the name of Adolph Hitler.

Hitler was born in 1889 in Braunau-am-Inn, on the Austrian shore of the Inn River. He enlisted in the Bavarian army, and during World War I received the Iron Cross. The small political party to which he belonged, whose name evoked both workers and socialism, was in reality a middle-class nationalist movement in favor of a strong central state and an education based on rigid military discipline. Anti-Semitism and anti-Marxism were two components of the NSDAP program, which sought to alienate elements perceived as opposed to nationalism. The positions on the party platform included a condemnation of the Treaty of Versailles and support for the unification (*Anschluss*) of Austria and the German State.

On November 8, 1923, Hitler and General Erich Ludendorff attempted a coup d'etat in Munich, known as the Beer Hall Putsch. Backed by a force of six hundred men, Hitler proclaimed the "national revolution" and took as captives the highest government officials of Bavaria. By the next day, the Bavarian police had the situation under control; they killed nineteen Nazis and forced others to flee, including Hitler, who was captured a short while later and sentenced to five years in prison in Landsberg, to the west of Munich. This is where he began to write *Mein Kampf*; after only nine months he was released on parole for "good conduct."

Germany was one step away from economic collapse. Hitler was beginning his rise and Bavaria was sinking ever deeper into the clutches of the right-wing nationalists.

The Country Policeman

Among the many in those years who were observing with concern and indignation the rise of Hitler and his collaborators in the heart of civilian Bavaria, was a deeply religious country policeman, Joseph Ratzinger. He was descended from a long line of Bavarian peasants.

In 1927 Ratzinger and his wife, Maria, settled in Marktl-am-Inn, a small village on the outskirts of Passau, not far from Austria and from Braunau-am-Inn, the hometown of Hitler. Their life unfolded far from the chaos of Munich and even farther from the many events in the rest of the world. The year began with a technological revolution, the first transoceanic telephone call from New York to London. The desire to cross the Atlantic and make the world smaller would be realized between May 20 and 21 of that same year when Charles Lindberg made the first nonstop solo flight from New York to Paris. On April 7, in the optimistic and high-flying America of the Roaring Twenties, which took no notice of the troubles brewing in the heart of Europe, the first long-distance transmission of an image had taken place: television was being born. One month later, in Los Angeles, came the birth of the Academy of Motion Picture Arts and Sciences, soon to become famous for its Oscar statuettes. In another part of the world, British troops were sent to China, provoking an uprising and hundreds of deaths. In the Middle East, Saudi Arabia proclaimed independence from the British Empire. Back in the United States, the Italian immigrants Sacco and Vanzetti were executed despite international protests. In the Soviet Union, Stalin succeeded in seizing total power by expelling Leon Trotsky from the Communist Party.

News of these events arrived—if it arrived at all—as distant echoes in the domestic tranquility of the Ratzinger family. On April 16, 1927, a brother joined Maria and Joseph's first two children, Georg and Maria. Joseph Alois Ratzinger was born on the afternoon of Holy Saturday, the day of the Easter vigil, at a house on number 11 Marktplatz, a yellow and white building with wooden shutters facing the market square. There has been a sign on the house commemorating the event since 1997.

His parents had him baptized that same day, in order to receive the newly blessed holy water of Easter. The neo-Gothic baptismal font used on the occasion would end up in the small city museum of Marktl-am-Inn decades later. "To be the first person baptized with the new water," Ratzinger wrote in his memoirs, "was seen as a significant act of Providence. I have always been filled with thanksgiving for having had my life immersed in this way in the Easter Mystery . . . the more I reflect on it, the more this seems fitting for the nature of our human life: we are still waiting for Easter; we are not yet standing in the full light but walking toward it full of trust."[1]

For the future Benedict XVI, it was always difficult to identify his true hometown. Although he was cradled in the warmth of a loving family, his youth was one of constant uprooting; he and his family moved from village to village in the rural areas of lower Bavaria. They moved often because of his father's work as a police commissioner.

With the passage of years, something would come to weigh on the mind of the father of the child who would become the successor of Peter. While nazism slowly took hold in Bavaria, the father's aversion to the militias also grew; to people of simple, solid faith like the Ratzingers, these militias were abhorrent.[2]

In 1929 the family moved to Tittmoning, a village on the Austrian border, where they would live for three years. They moved again in 1932. Profound changes had taken place since Joseph's birth. The Weimar Republic was on the verge of collapse. The Nazis were one step away from taking power on a national scale and had become the dominant force in Bavaria. In Munich, the first persecutions of the Jews had begun. The synagogues were targeted with growing frequency and anti-Semitism was on the rise.

Commissioner Ratzinger had begun to openly criticize the fanatics and the atmosphere surrounding the family had become unbearable. Joseph, Maria, and the children packed their bags and moved from Tittmoning to Aschau-am-Inn, at the foothills of the Alps. This was an exile of sorts that seems to have been provoked by the father's having spoken out one too many times to a local teacher in Tittmoning, an ardent Nazi who had tried to impose a pagan Maypole ritual on the village, which enraged the Catholic Ratzinger.[3] From Aschau the family would move again, in 1937, this time to Traunstein, where the future pope would spend most of his youth; it is the place he still considers his true hometown.

Four moves before the age of ten, in the ever-gloomier climate created by nazism—a reality so removed from the Catholic culture that had been nurtured in Lower Bavaria for centuries—probably had a profound impact on the development of Joseph Ratzinger's character. It definitely had a strong impact on the education he received from his parents. His mother worked as a cook, made soap at home to save money, and taught religious lessons to children, conveying to them a faith that must have appealed to her sons, Georg and Joseph, who both chose to enter the seminary a few years later. His father probably transferred to his namesake the heritage of one who defends the faith from the perils of modernity (the greatest of which, in that era, was unquestionably the rise of nazism).

In an interview with Vatican Radio shortly before his election as pope, Cardinal Ratzinger said, "I always remember very affectionately the profound goodness of my father and my mother, and naturally, for me, goodness means the capacity to say 'no,' because a goodness that allows everything does the other no good."[4] In these few short words, he outlines the creed of a lifetime, and perhaps provides a key for interpreting the positions that were the subject of such harsh criticism during his years at the Vatican as the prefect of the Congregation for the Doctrine of the Faith.

Traunstein

Central European culture made a deep impression on young Joseph. He was introduced to the music of Wolfgang Amadeus Mozart, which would become a lifelong passion. The piano proved to be a good friend that would accompany the future pope for decades; he is as much a virtuoso of the keyboard as he is of theology.

Yet this culture, too, was threatened by the rise of nazism. In September 1933, after Hitler came to power in Germany, the Reich created the Chamber of Culture, which had an iron grip over every form of art. From music to literature, painting, and theater, everything had to be examined by Hitler's propaganda chief, Joseph Goebbels. Performances of music by Jewish composers like Mendelssohn and Hindemith were banned. Men of culture who rebelled, like Thomas Mann, were forced into exile. In 1937, the same year the Ratzingers arrived in Traunstein, Hitler announced, "The end of the artistic folly and contamination of our people in art." [5]

The Ratzinger family was living on a nineteenth-century farm in Hufschlag, on the outskirts of Traunstein, in an area surrounded by an oak forest. Joseph Sr. was close to retirement at the same time as his children were commencing their scholastic careers. It was at the school in Traunstein that young Joseph discovered Latin and Greek, the first of the many foreign languages he would eventually learn. His early years at school (1937–39), however, also coincided with his first direct experience of the horrors of the Third Reich. In Stadtplatz, the central square in Traunstein, signs were put up calling for a boycott of Jewish businesses.[6] The worst was yet to come.

On the night of November 9–10, 1938, which would become known as Kristallnacht, the night of broken glass, the Nazis initiated the systematic destruction of the property and businesses owned by Jews throughout Germany. Approximately twenty thousand Jews were arrested, more than 180 synagogues were destroyed, and an estimated ninety-one Jews were murdered in the destructive fury.[7] The members of the small Jewish community in Traunstein were also subject to arrest and harassment.

Joseph's father, like the town's Catholic priest, watched the situation with a mounting horror. As the eldest son Georg has related, the Ratzinger family held firm to the conviction that only in the Church and its teachings was it possible to find refuge from such madness.[8] "No one doubted," Joseph Ratzinger wrote, "that the Church was the locus of all our hopes. Despite many human failings, the Church was the alternative to the destructive ideology of the [Nazi] rulers; in the inferno that had swallowed up the powerful, she had stood firm with a force coming to her from eternity. It had been demonstrated. The gates of hell will not prevail."[9]

In 1939, at the age of twelve, Joseph entered the minor seminary of Saint Michael, beginning the religious life that would lead him all the way to Saint Peter's. Georg had preceded him by a couple of years. "His report cards indicate that he was an outstanding student," according to Thomas Frauenlob, the current rector of the school. "He learned Latin, Greek, and Hebrew. But unlike his predecessor in the papacy, he was not very active in sports."[10] In another part of Europe, in Poland, a teenager by the name of Karol Wojtyla was distinguishing himself that same year in many sports, in addition to his academic talents, at the School of Philosophy of the Jagellonian University of Krakow.[11]

When Ratzinger was fourteen, in 1941, he became a member of the Hitler Youth, an episode that he never hid, although his detractors sometimes try to use it to cast a shadow over his reputation.[12] The testimony of the person directly involved, as well as of those who knew the reality of those years have demonstrated that membership was required; the decision was made for him by the heads of the seminary, and it was an obligation that no young boy in Hitler's Germany could avoid. Moreover, in the whole story of the Ratzinger family, there is no hint of Nazi sympathies.

Because he was a student at the seminary, Ratzinger soon received a waiver from attending the Hitler Youth meetings. In the meantime, the chaos of World War II began, and not even the gates of the seminary could protect him from being called to arms.

3. FROM THE HORRORS
TO THE ALTAR

Joseph, the Soldier

The student Joseph Ratzinger must present himself on August 2, 1943, at nine o'clock A.M. in the courtyard in front of the school. From there he will be transported together with others to the combat post assigned to him."[1]

The letter arrived at the end of July 1943, in the Traunstein seminary, and was dated July 26. In Italy, Benito Mussolini had just fallen, while the Allies were closing in on the Nazi regime, which had reached the peak of its power in 1942. Hitler needed any men he could get, including teenage boys. The tone of the letter and especially the eagle of the Reich stamped on the top left no alternative.

While he succeeded in getting a waiver from the Hitler Youth because of his studies, it was not possible for the seventeen-year-old Ratzinger to escape the order to enlist sent not only to him, but also to all of his schoolmates at Saint Michael seminary. He was given a Wehrmacht uniform and the assignment of defending a BMW factory in southern Bavaria. At the beginning, he was given leave three times a week to continue his studies at the Maximilians Gymnasium of Munich, a privilege that would not last long.

The unit to which he was assigned was the Flak, the nickname for the Fliegerabwehrkanonen, the anti-aircraft artillery weapons that Germany produced in massive quantities in those years and that were used for various purposes. The lightest units had 12.7-mm machine guns and 20-mm light cannons that could be quickly moved to form a defense perimeter in the event of air raids, convoys, or military installations; there were also 37-mm ones. Flaks, more powerful and less mobile, were quickly upgraded to radar capacity for help in aiming. By 1942 Germany had deployed fifteen thousand 88-mm cannons in Flak defense lines that reached as far as Holland.

Ratzinger would later write that he did not fire a single shot during the period of his military service.[2] In the months he spent protecting the BMW factory he witnessed firsthand one of the horrors of nazism: detainees from the nearby Dachau concentration camp—where hundreds of thousands of prisoners passed between 1933 and 1945—were brought in to perform the most menial jobs. The number of Jews who died in Dachau is not known, and the people who ended up in the camp belonged to every religious and ethnic group—they were imprisoned there on political and religious grounds.

In September 1944 Joseph was sent home to Traunstein for a brief stay, but he was recalled for a new assignment. As a soldier Ratzinger found himself under the command and the injustices/ harassment of the Austrian Legion, a group that was notorious in Bavaria for its violence. "There were fanatical ideologues who bullied us relentlessly," the future pope would later write.[3] While he was working on antitank traps, Ratzinger often saw long processions of Hungarian Jews who had been captured by the Germans and were on their way to the death camps.

On April 16, 1945, after his eighteenth birthday, the time came for basic military training with the German infantry. With him were thirty- and forty-year-old men; any man who could carry a rifle was conscripted in a desperate attempt to defend the indefensible. Germany was one step away from collapse, and the Reich had reached the end of the line. The German soldiers knew that it was only a matter of time before what remained of Hitler's military power would fall apart; some of them became increasingly reckless.

At his young age, Joseph Ratzinger made a rash decision that could have cost him his life. He deserted.[4] With his uniform still on, he left his unit and started to walk home. However, his path soon crossed that of a patrol of the much-feared SS. He was convinced that he was done for. He knew all too well what happened to deserters like him. The SS had no qualms about summary executions of any man they captured who had left his combat post. Sometimes they even hung the deserter from a nearby lamppost, as an example to anyone who might be considering the idea.

But it seems that Providence intervened. The SS looked at his arm and saw that it was bandaged because of a recently acquired injury. "You're wounded, go on ahead," they told him. He had escaped danger.

The former soldier was soon at home in the arms of his parents. He had returned to Traunstein, but he wouldn't be there for long.

It was May 1945. The Americans had arrived in Bavaria. When they entered Traunstein, they went from house to house; this included the Ratzinger's. They determined that Joseph was a German soldier. They made him put on his uniform again and then ordered him to march to the central square holding his arms in the air.

Other German soldiers were rounded up as well, forming a sizeable group of prisoners of war. The prevailing feeling among the soldiers was exhaustion.

The prisoners formed a line and were told to start walking. The soldiers walked for three days on roads that had once been used by the heavy vehicles of the German military. Now the roads were deserted and quiet. The image that has remained imprinted on Ratzinger's memory is that of other prisoners feeding into the long procession and becoming a river of men who were defeated but grateful to be alive. "The Americans were taking pictures," he wrote, "especially the younger ones, so that they would have a souvenir of the defeated army and its discouraged men."

Joseph spent weeks in a barb-wire-enclosed outdoor cage the Americans had built for the prisoners. On June 19 they released him. A truck driver who was transporting milk gave him a ride all the way to Traunstein.

At home, the hugs of Josef and Maria Ratzinger were tempered by lingering concern. They were overjoyed by Joseph's return but worried about his older brother. Georg had turned twenty-one and had also been a soldier. The family hadn't received any news from him since April and was very apprehensive about his whereabouts.

In mid-July Georg suddenly reappeared; he was unharmed. After hugging everybody Georg began to cry and to intone, *Grosser Gott, wir Loben Dich*, "Mighty God, we praise you," an eighteenth-century Viennese hymn of thanks to the Lord written by Ignaz Franz. Joseph, his sister, and then their parents joined in the chorus.[5]

The war was finally over for the Ratzinger family. The months that followed, in domestic tranquility and post-war calm, would be remembered by the future pope as, "one of the happiest times of my life."

Back at the Seminary

Georg and Joseph Ratzinger were finally going to be able to return to their studies. They were two boys who had lived their entire adolescence during one of the worst wars of history. They had seen the evil that men can do, but they had also started to see that suffering, the horrors and sin of it, are not the last word on man's fate. Even the Nazis, who had seemed invincible, had been swept away. The solid education they received from their parents had proven to be true. "The gates of hell will not prevail."

In remembering their years at the seminary, Georg Ratzinger would say, "The sensation that we experienced together, as brothers, was that of being in God, the awareness of entering the family created by God and by Christ. The thought that resided in our young minds was that it was a choice for our whole life that would accompany our every act and decision." [6] This was a path they had chosen together when they were little, "as early as elementary school: we lived in a small village, thinking of values, of love, of what was good."

While following a path parallel to Georg's, the young Joseph nurtured above all his ties to his older sister, Maria, who became one of the central figures in his life and who lived in Rome alongside her brother, the prefect of the Congregation for the Doctrine of the Faith, until her death in 1991.

The Ratzinger brothers returned to the seminary in November 1945. In the large, imposing white building, on a hilltop overlooking the center of Traunstein, Georg and Joseph prayed, studied, socialized with their schoolmates, and slept in the bunk beds of the vast common room. These are the years when the man who would be pope solidified his passion for literature and music.

In 1947, Ratzinger transferred to the Herzogliches Georgianum, an ancient Bavarian theological institute in Munich, to continue his studies. The school was founded in 1494 and was associated with the University of Munich. Here he was totally immersed in theology and philosophy, receiving excellent grades and standing out due to his lively intellect. Here, too, his character as a future priest would mature. The seminarian's education for the priesthood was divided between the Georgianum and the Higher School of Philosophy and Theology at Freising.[7] It was in Freising that Joseph began the ecclesiastical journey that would lead him first to Munich, then to the Congregation for the Doctrine of the Faith in Rome, and then, on a spring day inside the Sistine Chapel, to election as the supreme leader of the Catholic Church.

Freising

Today a city of thirty-six thousand inhabitants to the north of Munich, Freising is one of the oldest towns in Bavaria. Saint Corbinian first announced the Christian faith there in the eighth century. The local diocese was founded by Saint Boniface in 738.

Distinguishing features of Freising are the two bell towers of the Cathedral of Saint Mary and Saint Corbinian, which was consecrated in 1250 after a previous building, a Romanesque basilica, was destroyed by fire in 1159. The cathedral had long been a point of reference and prayer for Joseph Ratzinger, who spent years of study and teaching in the medieval atmosphere of Freising. It is not hard to imagine the young Ratzinger wandering around the cloister decorated with the stuccowork of Johann Baptist Zimmermann, immersed in the books of the local baroque library or admiring the Romanesque elegance of the crypt that held the remains of Saint Corbinian beneath the cathedral.

Many years later the saint would inspire the emblem of Ratzinger, who became archbishop of Munich and Freising. It is said that one day Saint Corbinian was on the road to Rome when he came across a bear attacking the horse that was carrying his baggage. Furious, he ordered the animal to carry the bundle as far as Rome. At journey's end, the saint freed the bear that had worked for him. A bear became Ratzinger's emblem.

It is harder to know what Ratzinger might have thought about one of the many columns supporting the crypt dedicated to the saint. The famous pillar of the beast, whose delicately carved figures depicted the battle of Christianity against evil, was represented by crocodile-like monsters.

Georg and Joseph Ratzinger were ordained as priests in the cathedral on June 29, 1951, on the feast of the apostles Peter and Paul, in a ceremony celebrated by the archbishop of Munich, Cardinal Michael von Faulhaber.[8]

Father Joseph would stay in Freising, the spiritual heart of Bavaria, for a while. One year after becoming a priest, he returned to the school from which he had graduated as a student, but this time as a teacher.

In 1953 he received his doctorate in theology from the University of Munich, with a thesis entitled *The People and House of God in Saint Augustine's Doctrine of the Church*. Two great German theologians of the period, Gottlieb Söhngen and Michael Schmaus, were on the committee that heard the twenty-six-year-old Ratzinger's defense of his work.[9]

Four years later, Söhngen, a professor of fundamental theology at Munich, would again supervise Father Joseph at his university teaching qualification exam when he presented *Theology in the History of Saint Bonaventure.*

After impressing the most important theologians of Bavaria with his intellect, Joseph Ratzinger became a professor of dogma and fundamental theology at the Higher School of Freising; he was thirty years old.

The signs of a great career in the making were clear.

4. MUSIC AND BEAUTY

Mozart and Dostoyevsky

The theological studies that absorbed Joseph Ratzinger in the 1950s did not keep him away from his other passions, primarily his love for music. Indeed, it was in this period that the future pope's strong conviction that beauty is one of the most powerful ways to Christ was solidified.

Mozart and classical music were potent inspirations to the thirty-year-old Ratzinger, comparable to that attained from reading Saint Augustine or Saint Bonaventure. "Beauty is knowledge," he would say years later, as a continuation of those early ideas from his Freising years, "a higher form of knowledge, since it strikes man with all the grandeur of truth."[1]

In the years when he would be the leader of the Congregation for the Doctrine of the Faith, Ratzinger would be given a label, borrowed from the pages of the *Brothers Karamazov*, by his adversaries. They would call him the Grand Inquisitor. However, it was not that grim figure but rather another passage from Dostoyevsky that would captivate Ratzinger, a sentence he would often quote: "Beauty will save us."

Surrounded by the medieval architecture of Freising and continuing to immerse himself in the music of Central European culture, as he had since his childhood, with his beloved Mozart music in his head, the young professor thus laid the foundations of his passion for beauty that he would later express in future sermons and reflections. In a message to the Communion and Liberation meeting in Rimini, given in 2002, he said:

> *True knowledge is being struck by the arrow of beauty that wounds man, moved by reality, how it is Christ himself who is present and in an ineffable way disposes and forms the souls of men. Being struck and overcome through the beauty of Christ is a more real, more profound knowledge than mere rational deduction. Of course we must not underrate the importance of theological reflection, of exact and precise theological thought; it remains absolutely necessary. But to move from here to disdain or reject the impact produced by the response of the heart in the encounter with beauty as a true form of knowledge would impoverish us and dry up our faith and our theology. We must rediscover this form of knowledge; it is a pressing need of our time.*

The theologian, who prepared to immerse himself in the complex period of the 1960s—to address the issues raised by the Second Vatican Ecumenical Council and then to clash with university students during the uprisings of 1968, when the authority of Rome was questioned—would maintain intact the love of beauty that he had cultivated in his boyhood amid the pastoral scenery of rural Bavaria. Mozart's music had left its mark.

"Music, after all," he would say in the late 1990s, "has the power to bring people together. . . . Art is elemental. Reason alone as it's expressed in the sciences, can't be man's complete answer to reality, and it can't express everything that man can, wants to, and has to express. I think God built this into man." [2]

Over the years, Ratzinger would come to speak of music more and more with the tone of voice of a lover. This was the case, for example, of an anecdote he told in his Rimini message of an "unforgettable experience" in Munich. It was after the sudden death of the conductor Karl Richter, one of the greatest interpreters of Bach, and he was listening to a concert conducted by Leonard Bernstein dedicated to the memory of the deceased artist. The program, of course, was Bach, and when the performance concluded triumphantly, Ratzinger turned to the Lutheran Bishop Hanselmann, who was sitting next him, and said enthusiastically, "Anyone who has heard this, knows that faith is true."

Von Balthasar

While Ratzinger acquired his passion for musical beauty from his parents, it was through Hans Urs von Balthasar, a fellow theologian, that beauty would become one the themes that most fascinated the future Benedict XVI. Few people seem to have had an influence on Ratzinger comparable to that exercised by his friendship with Balthasar, which was destined to develop in the 1960s. It is not hard to guess the reasons why, when one looks at the passions the two theologians shared.

"Mozart is my North Star," Balthasar used to say. [3] To reinforce the concept, one day he gave away his stereo system and all his records by the Austrian composer, explaining that he didn't need them anymore since he already knew all of them by heart.

The man who French Jesuit Henri de Lubac, another influence on Ratzinger, called "perhaps the best educated mind of our times," was born in 1905 in Lucerne, Switzerland, to a family whose devotion was very different from that of the Ratzingers. At the age of thirty, after being struck as if by lightning one day in the Black Forest, Balthasar felt that he had been called and decided to begin a novitiate with the Jesuits, which set him on the path to the religious life. He received his degree years earlier with top honors; now he buried himself in studies ranging over every aspect of human knowledge.

In later decades he became a well-respected author, who penned more than one thousand books and articles. Although he was not invited to the Second Vatican Council, in the years to come he gained the recognition of popes, especially John Paul II, and in 1988 the pontiff nominated him as a cardinal. Two days before the ceremony in which he would have received the cap, however, Balthasar died while preparing to celebrate the morning mass. Cardinal Ratzinger presided at his funeral mass, dedicating a deeply moving homily to his friend.

"Beauty is the word that should be our first," the Swiss theologian used to repeat, in harmony with the younger Ratzinger.[4] For Balthasar, too, pleasures of music were not purely aesthetic. In 1987, when he received the Wolfgang Amadeus Mozart Prize in Innsbruck, he said, "My youth was defined by music. As a student in Vienna I delighted in the last of the romantics—Wagner, Strauss, and especially Mahler. That all came to an end once I had Mozart in my ears. To this day he has never left those ears."[5]

From this shared passion a strong bond would develop between Ratzinger and Balthasar, within a Church that was moving toward ruptures and clashes. First, however, there were other steps to be completed, especially that of the Second Vatican Ecumenical Council.

5. THE COUNCIL YEARS

Professor Ratzinger

The intellectual prestige of Joseph Ratzinger would grow in the late 1950s. The young professor took multiple approaches to the theological issues that were the focus of his research. His point of view as a scholar was being formed—which he would describe years later as Augustinian—as were his thoughts on the relationship between faith and religion and his *Credo ut intelligam, intelligo ut credam* (I believe to understand, and I understand to believe). Ratzinger might have said that he was also indebted to Plato, "in the sense that the memory of God is implanted in man,"[1] but he might also have indicated authors such as Thomas More, John Henry Newman, and Dietrich Bonhoeffer as influences. The teachings of Saint Benedict, the way in which the saint became the leader of a new Christian culture in a Europe that had been overrun by barbarians, was another essential point of reference that would be strengthened over the decades; it inspired him to introduce himself to the world, as pope, with the name of the patron saint of Europe.

In 1959, an important year in Ratzinger's life, his activity and fame would spread beyond Bavaria to the rest of Germany. A new assignment arrived for Ratzinger: an academic chair in Bonn.

While in Munich, a deep friendship developed between Ratzinger and Hubert Luthe, who at the time was the secretary of the archbishop of Cologne, Cardinal Josef Frings. It was through Luthe that the cardinal came to know and appreciate the work of the young theologian. His esteem opened doors at the university of the then-capital of western Germany, where Ratzinger taught fundamental theology from 1959 to 1963. As his colleagues from those years recalled after his election to the papacy, the central point of Ratzinger's teaching was, "that God had revealed himself through Jesus Christ." [2]

His first residence in Bonn was at the Collegium Albertinum. Later he moved to a private house in Bad Godesberg, on 11 Wurzerstrasse. During this period Ratzinger began to lay the foundation for his first book, which would make him famous in the Catholic world. Published in 1968, *Introduction to Christianity* is a collection of his university lectures on the profession of the apostolic faith. In the university atmosphere of Bonn, Ratzinger gave lectures that focused on the questions of God and of Christ, and that illustrated that the Catholic Church is the place for faith. He provided a contemporary interpretation of the Apostles' Creed that he hoped would resonate. The book unites the fundamental truths to a profound religious reflection, accompanied by a masterly knowledge of the Scriptures and of the history of theology. The solid academic approach of the book was combined with an ability to explain the faith in an accessible way that everyone could understand. It even incorporated subtle humor, which contrasts with the stiff image associated with Ratzinger in recent years.

Introduction to Christianity has had a profound impact on the international Catholic debate as well as on the personal conversion of men and women throughout the world. According to Monsignor Lorenzo Albacete, a professor of theology at Saint Joseph's Seminary in New York and a well-regarded writer and commentator:

The first time that I heard talk of Joseph Ratzinger was in 1968, the year of the great tumult. I was a young and restless Catholic scientist who found himself suddenly surrounded by people who were amazed at the fact that I could be a good scientist and at the same time claim to believe in transcendence. I never had a good answer to their questions and knew that it was necessary to find an intelligent response to these objections. I started to look for texts that could help me with this task, and I found this book by Ratzinger, Introduction to Christianity. *That book changed my life. It was like looking at Christianity for the first time, through new eyes. Ratzinger practically invited us to make scorched earth of what we thought we knew about Christianity and to take a new look at it, starting from scratch.*[3]

In the book Ratzinger took as his starting point the Apostles' Creed, analyzing the foundations of the Christian message beginning with God the Father, moving on to the figure of Jesus Christ, and finally the Trinity. A consistent theme of the book is the relevance of the Christian message for modern man in the framework of the Church. Although the groundwork for *Introduction* was laid in Bonn, some years would pass before it saw the light. In the meantime, Ratzinger lived through the thrilling experience of participating in a Council.

Toward Vatican II

Joseph Ratzinger arrived at the threshold of the 1960s with the direct experience of totalitarianism behind him and another type of totalitarianism still present. In the Hitler years, he had been able to see firsthand man's capacity for distorting the truth and to see the dire consequences of lies: the extermination of the Jews, the Third Reich's mad scientific research, the myth of the Aryan race.

Once nazism ended, Ratzinger found himself living in a Germany split in two, where Catholic friends and colleagues who had remained in the East were forced to bear the impositions of another form of totalitarianism, communism. This reality made him increasingly aware of the fact that the Church was something other, called upon to resist the waves of the moment and remain firmly anchored to its traditions, to the foundations of the faith. To Christ.

These convictions were hardly new in his life. In essence, he was remaining faithful to the teachings of his father and to the simple faith of his mother, to their "profound goodness." [4] For Ratzinger, it became clearer that the Church had to propose alternatives to the dominant culture, to anchor itself to its absolute truths, if it wished to protect the freedom of man and escape from totalitarianism.

Ratzinger's parents, who had been so important in forging the character of the future pope, both died during this period, within a few years of each other. Joseph Sr., the former Bavarian policeman, died on August 23, 1959. Four years later, on December 16, 1963, his mother, Maria, died at age seventy-five.

Maria, daughter of a peasant couple who lived in the province of Bolzano, Italy, Anton Peintner and Maria Taubner, was born on January 8, 1884, in a small house near a mill in Rio Pusteria, in the Alto Adige region. This is a part of Italy in the foothills of the Alps that has historically always gravitated more toward the Tirolese area and central Europe than toward Italy's Mediterranean culture. The Peintners lost their house in a flood and probably decided to move elsewhere to seek their fortune; they chose Bavaria. Yet these

Pusteria roots remained close to Ratzinger's heart; several times over the years he visited the graves of his ancestors on his mother's side.[5]

The loss of their parents further strengthened the bonds and affection between the Ratzinger siblings, especially between Joseph and his sister. But their paths were separate and it was clear that the youngest child of Joseph and Maria was embarking on a career that would take him very far.

The Germany in which the future pope was making a name for himself as a theologian was that of Konrad Adenauer, the first chancellor of the republic, who was in power from 1949 to 1963. His was an era of political moderation that helped Germany to slowly regain its standing in Europe and to erase the ignominy of nazism, and that offered a tough opposition to the Soviet Union and its satellite, East Germany.

At the Vatican, Pope Pius XII died on October 28, 1958, and was succeeded by the seventy-seven-year-old Cardinal Angelo Roncalli, who took the name Pope John XXIII. His age led many to consider him from the start a transitional pontificate—a notion that has been repeated recently regarding the seventy-eight-year-old Ratzinger. But from the start, Pope Roncalli let it be known that he would leave his mark on the Church and on history.

Among the many legacies left by John XXIII, the most significant was undoubtedly the convocation of the Second Vatican Ecumenical Council, known as Vatican II. The announcement was made at the basilica of Saint Paul on the outskirts of Rome on April 25, 1959. After consultations with many advisors, above all with the secretary of state, Cardinal Tardini, the pope himself made the decision.

What the pope was asking of the members of the Council, which opened in Rome on October 11, 1962, was not to define new truths for the Church but rather to identify ways of espousing the traditional doctrine that would speak to a modern sensibility and to the historical context. The word that John XXIII used to describe this need for renewal was *aggiornamento*, an updating.

At the behest of John XXIII, the Council's aggiornamento had to address the whole life of the Church, with special attention to the issues of mercy and communication with the world: it was not a question of issuing condemnations or proposing an ecclesiastical wall against various aspects of modernity, but rather of embracing humanity with a language and gestures that were closer to a twentieth-century sensibility. In the context of the dialogue, an opening to those of other Christian faiths, who had been invited to participate in the Council, was also a goal.[6]

Pope John XXIII set the rhythm of the Council's works and encouraged diverse viewpoints to be shared, making clear that he wanted deliberations and not just words. He would not live to see the conclusion, however, because he died on June 3, 1963. In addition to the Council, whose work was well underway, he also left behind a final encyclical, *Pacem in terris* (1963), in which he gave voice to the need for peace at a time when it seemed to be more at risk than ever before. During the Cuban Missile Crisis of fall 1962, the pope had intervened by sending a strong message at a moment when the threat of a nuclear war breaking out between the United States and the Soviet Union seemed possible. In 1961 a wall was erected in Berlin; for years it would be a physical manifestation of the deep divisions in Europe.

John XXIII died at a historic moment—the world was filled with tension that was further increased five months after his death by the assassination of the American president, John F. Kennedy.

The *Peritus*

The new pope—Giovanni Battista Montini—was elected on June 21, 1963; he chose the name Paul VI. His first message to the world contained the promise to continue the work of John XXIII. Within the first years of his papacy, one of the crucial questions he had to deal with was the request from those at the periphery of the Holy See for greater collegiality, a greater involvement of the bishops in the administration of the Church. This issue also emerged in the Council's discussions, together with the often provocative requests for change that came from some of the members of the Council's assemblies.

Paul VI brought the Council to a close in December 1965, after four working sessions in which more than 2,200 bishops, about 300 experts, and many observers from other churches had participated. The outcome of the Council was that Paul VI issued four constitutions: on the Church, the revelation, the liturgy, and relations between the Church and the contemporary world. He decided on a series of steps that were meant to move the inner transformation of the Church in the direction requested by the Council. Among the most significant: the creation of an Episcopal synod to assist the work of the pope, in which representatives of bishops from throughout the world would participate; the establishment of national bishops' conferences; the formation of parishioner and pastoral councils in the dioceses; and the transformation of the old Holy Office into the Congregation for the Doctrine of the Faith.

The man who would later guide this institution, Joseph Ratzinger, was able to come to Rome in the Council years because he was picked by Cardinal Frings of Cologne, who had already supported him for the Bonn professorship. During the first part of Ratzinger's life, the figure of Cardinal Frings undoubtedly had an influence comparable to that held by Cardinal Faulhaber of Munich. Faulhaber is not only the man who ordained the Ratzinger brothers to the priesthood, but it seems that he also played a part in the original decision of the future pope to dedicate his life to the Church. One day in 1932 a limousine pulled up in the Bavarian village where they were living. Out stepped Cardinal Faulhaber, wrapped in his archbishop's vestments, an impressive figure both fascinating and unusual for the inhabitants of the small rural town. Joseph, who was five, was overwhelmed. That night he told his father he wanted to be a cardinal. Recalled Georg, "It wasn't so much the car, because we weren't the types to be impressed by technology. It was the way in which the cardinal appeared, his bearing, the clothes he was wearing; the whole thing had made a great impression on him."[7] That day, according to the pope's brother, little Joseph set aside the initial idea of becoming a painter and instead decided on a career as a cardinal.

Little could the Bavarian child know of the enormous difficulties that Faulhaber was encountering trying to reconcile his role as the archbishop of Bavaria with the rise of the Nazis, who saw the Catholic Church as a dangerous enemy. Historians are divided in their judgment of the Munich cardinal, but he was faulted for what many have seen as his fainthearted resistance to Hitler's ideas.

When Cardinal Frings was putting together a delegation to travel to the Council, he immediately thought of Ratzinger, who he asked to be his main *peritus*, or consultant. The thoughts and words of the thirty-five-year-old Ratzinger, acting as a ghostwriter, were behind the theses that Frings presented to the Roman Curia in 1962, including harsh criticism of the Congregation for the

Doctrine of the Faith, which he accused of being a "source of scandal."[8] Powerful cardinals such as Ottaviani and Siri were listening. So was Cardinal Montini, who would become pope the next year. The future Paul VI was impressed by Ratzinger's ideas and by the authority he demonstrated despite his relative youth. Some of the theses he proposed to Rome were bold, such as his comment that, "God, throughout the entire historical process, has never been on the side of the institutions, but always on the side of the suffering, the persecuted."[9]

Years later, Paul VI recognized the intellectual prominence of Ratzinger, first by nominating him as the archbishop of Munich and then by making him a cardinal.

The Council years marked Professor Ratzinger's emergence on the international ecclesiastic and academic scene. Not long thereafter he would be given, in addition to his chair at Bonn, a professorship at the University of Münster, which he would hold from 1963 to 1966. In 1966 he received another prestigious post, at the University of Tübingen.

Ratzinger's life was about to reach another turning point.

6. NINETEEN SIXTY-EIGHT

Tübingen

They call it the "city of the learned," a fame that it undoubtedly deserves. The list of important people who have studied there is long: the poets Hölderin, Hauff, and Mörike, and the philosophers Hegel and Schelling, just to name a few. Tübingen is a relatively small city, with approximately eighty-five thousand inhabitants, and a student population that exceeds twenty thousand. A school of Catholic theology has long coexisted, without tensions but within the academic dialogue, with the Protestant institutions on campus.

The epicenter of life in Tübingen is the Eberhard-Karls University, whose history dates back to 1477. That was the year that Eberhard im Bart, a count and later a duke of Württemberg, decided to create a university center for southwest Germany, not far from Stuttgart, inspired by a 1468 pilgrimage to Jerusalem. Upon his return from the Holy Land, the count chose a new motto for his life, "I shall try," and decided that his vocation from that moment forth would be to help young people, "from every corner of the world" to combat and extinguish "the pernicious fire of human ignorance and blindness."[1]

When the thirty-nine-year-old Ratzinger arrived in Tübingen, in the Baden-Württemberg region, he was fascinated by the beauty of the place: the sixteenth-century castle of Hohentübingen, the Gothic Stiftskirche, and the Tower of Hölderlin on the Neckar River were a feast for the eyes and the heart of a lover of beauty like Ratzinger. But his joy over the place where he had been called to teach was short-lived.

The driving force behind getting the University of Tübingen to hire Ratzinger as a professor of theology was a Swiss colleague, Hans Küng, who had arrived in the university town in 1960 after leaving Paris's Sorbonne to take the chair in fundamental theology. Younger than Ratzinger by one year, Küng was a superstar in the theological world of the 1960s. Pope John XXIII had summoned him to Rome as his own peritus during the Council, and his ideas had considerable influence on the conciliar works. In Rome he had come to respect and enjoy the friendship of Ratzinger, who together with Küng, the Flemish Dominican Edward Schillebeeckx, and the Jesuit Karl Rahner were part of a small group of progressive theologians that was closely followed in ecclesiastical and especially university circles.

The friendship between Ratzinger and Küng carried no hint of the future epic clash between the two. In Tübingen, in the first years of Ratzinger's tenure there, it was in all probability impossible to predict their bitter theological conflict in later years, which would lead Küng to apply to his former friend the label that has been used by detractors of the theologian. According to Küng, "Joseph Ratzinger is frightened, and like Dostoyevsky's Grand Inquisitor, there is nothing he fears more than freedom."[2]

In April 2005, when the man whom he had compared to the Grand Inquisitor appeared on the balcony overlooking Saint Peter's

Square to a crowd chanting his new name—"Be-ne-dict! Be-ne-dict!"—Küng did not hide his feelings. "The election of Cardinal Ratzinger to the papacy is an enormous disappointment to all those who hoped in a reformist, pastoral pope . . . But we must wait and see, because experience shows that the papacy, in the Catholic Church of today, is a challenge that can change anyone: he who enters the conclave as a progressive cardinal can come out a conservative pope . . . he who enters as a conservative cardinal could come out as a progressive pope."[3]

"Progressive" and "conservative" are categories that have been used for years to characterize the theological factions that began to break out in Tübingen. Ratzinger was numbered among the progressives because of his passion for theological freedom and his criticisms, which helped lead the Roman Curia to greater openness and support for freedom of expression. Looking back at his personal history, however, one can see that he was exhorting anything but a kind of Catholic anarchy. Christ remained at the center of his reflections and the Church remained the definite place of the faith, as it had been in his younger years in the midst of the Nazi hatred, and as it continued to be in the midst of the Cold War and the confrontation with the Communist bloc that kept his Germany split in two.

When the climate heated up at Tübingen, as at other universities throughout the world with the student protests of 1968, Ratzinger did not recognize any of the instances of change that he had theorized. The revolt that penetrated even the ancient, austere halls of the university founded by Count Eberhard left him troubled, disappointed, and confused. "Manifestations of a brutal, cruel, tyrannical ideology," is how Ratzinger described what took place at the university where he was teaching.[4]

Reflections on the Protests

In Germany, the students became leaders of the movement that had spilled over from the massive uprisings in France in May, and the universities quickly became cauldrons of protest and rebellion. In later years, Ratzinger returned to these events repeatedly, severely criticizing them. In 1999, while speaking about the flourishing of Catholic movements in the late 1960s, he explained that he, too, had encountered the new realities of that difficult period and to have thus had, "The joy and the grace of seeing young Christians touched by the force of the Holy Spirit." In a moment of weakness that has been called, "the winter of the Church," he added, "the Holy Spirit created a new spring. It was also a response to the two negative experiences that had been lived in Germany: in the academic world, where theology took its distance from an enthusiastic faith, in order to be completely equal to other disciplines, thereby becoming 'coldly scientific,' reduced to a phenomenon that oppressed faith through unilateral reasoning; and in the Church, in order to feed a growing bureaucracy." [5]

On that same occasion, he identified 1968 as a harmful period, the consequences of which continued to be felt:

After 1968 there was an explosion of secularism that radicalized a process that had been underway for two-hundred years: the Christian foundation has diminished. We are thinking of the fact that until forty years ago a law that treated a homosexual union almost as if it were a marriage would have been unthinkable. Now we must reformulate our reasons in order to regain the conscience of men today and we must accept a conflict of values, hence we must defend man, not only the Church, as the Pope wrote in many of his encyclicals. In the face of secularization, to be contemporary to the man of today we must not, however, lose our contemporaneity to the Church of all times . . . In our times we note a certain prevalence of the Protestant spirit in a cultural sense, because protest against the past seems to be modern and to better respond to the present. This is why, on our part, we need to show that Catholicism bears the heredity of the past and the future, even if it does so against the tides of these times.[6]

A few years earlier, in 1993, Ratzinger had reprised the issue of 1968 when he presented a collection of writings by Father Luigi Giussani, founder of Communion and Liberation (CL), one of the new Catholic movements to which he liked to refer when he spoke of the "joy and the grace of seeing young Christians touched by the force of the Holy Spirit," which he had felt in observing the movements in the midst of the protest years. Wrote Ratzinger:

A decisive step in the struggle [of Father Giussani] was the confrontation with the spirit of utopia, forced by the events of 1968. We remember: the better future world suddenly became the sole object of faith. Or better: there was no more "object of faith," but rather only the projection of a hope, which in its turn signified action. Even Christians stopped talking about redemption through the cross, about the resurrection of Jesus Christ, and about our hope in eternal life. They, too, came to speak almost only of our society, of the better civilization that would be born. Utopia became the only dogma that inspired thought and action.

For Ratzinger, it was fascinating to see how in the Church ideas were emerging, like the movements, that instead of utopia spoke of the "presence." In the same 1993 text, he also noted:

The all-dominant utopia was unmasked as an empty phantom: staring at the void in a dreamy state, we lose sight of reality. Christianity is presence, the here and now of the Lord, who drives us into the here and now of the faith and the life of the faith. In this way the true alternative becomes clear: Christianity is not theory, or moralism, or ritualism, but rather a happening, an encounter with a presence, with a God who has entered into history and will continue to enter into it.[7]

7. HANS, HENRI, AND JOSEPH

Return to Bavaria

Tübingen could not long remain the place where Ratzinger exercised his academic activity. The agitated atmosphere of the student protests was at odds with his character, which has been described as gentle and reserved. Face to face with the "dominant utopia," Ratzinger decided to distance himself—not only from Tübingen but also from the progressive theologians, including Küng, Schillebeeckx, and Rahner, to whom he had been linked.

He no longer agreed with their ideas, and felt that the spirit of Vatican II had been betrayed. In the effort to adapt itself to modern man, Catholic thinking had decided to compromise its foundations. This, more than anything else, could absolutely not be accepted.

During his lectures, the auditorium was always packed with students who heard him speak of the aesthetics of the liturgy and the papal primacy over the Church. Young people, who nicknamed him "Goldmund," [1] golden mouth, because of his eloquence, were entranced by his approach but put off by his conclusions. He found himself increasingly isolated in the academic world.

In 1969 Ratzinger abandoned his teaching post in Tübingen to return to Bavaria. In a letter he bid farewell to Küng, who had been his sponsor and had urged him to come to terms with the students, with whom he was no longer able to communicate. The man who succeeded him in Tübingen was Walter Kasper, who would also become a cardinal and one of the electors of Benedict XVI.

The next school to welcome Ratzinger was the University of Regensburg. In making the move away from the small city of Tübingen, he would not have to sacrifice his aesthetic sense. Regensburg is the medieval jewel of Germany and its location, overlooking the Danube in one of the most scenic parts of Bavaria, has inspired artists for centuries. "Regensburg is located in such a beautiful manner that its area was bound to attract a city," said one of the giants of German literature in 1786, Johann von Goethe, who loved it.[2] In this city dominated by the great cathedral of Saint Peter, Ratzinger found himself once again immersed in the comfortable climate of his native Bavaria, enriched by physical manifestations of a history that dated as far back as the Romans. There were no lack of reminders of the tragedy of the Holocaust as well, which had a deep impact on the region; for example, this is where Oskar Schindler, best known to the world thanks to the 1993 film *Schindler's List*, lived much of his life.

Ratzinger was given the chair in dogma and history of dogma in Regensburg. He would maintain his association with the university—becoming vice president—even after he received higher ecclesiastical assignments. As further testimony to his attachment to the city, he decided to build a house here in 1970[3]—an unusual choice for a man who spent his life moving between teachers' housing, bishops' residences, and apartments in the Roman Curia.

The house that Ratzinger built in Regensburg was a simple dwelling on a quiet street on the outskirts of town, with an enclosed garden planted with rose bushes and decorated with two statues: one of the Virgin Mary, the other of a cat, his favorite pet. Ratzinger lived there until 1977, when Pope Paul VI called him to become archbishop of Munich and Freising, which had so impressed him as a child, when he first met Cardinal Faulhaber. Yet he would continue to return to Regensburg in later years for periods of rest, even after he made his final move to Rome. When Ratzinger was elected pope there were celebrations in the town, and his neighbors spoke of their relations with this unassuming resident, who nevertheless was pleased to accept their dinner invitations when he happened to be in town.

Rupert Hafbauer, who is a next-door neighbor of the pope's, tells the following story. "Once he came with us to visit the beekeepers' club to which I belong, and he was fascinated to observe the bees. At a certain point the cardinal pointed to the queen bee and said, 'You see the power of females in society!'"[4]

Accustomed to the life of the itinerant scholar and the many changes of residence entailed, as soon as he was elected pope Benedict XVI decided not to move immediately to the papal residence or to a building inside the Vatican City, traditionally the temporary home of the newly elected pontiff while he awaits preparation of his apartment in the Apostolic Palace. Instead, he chose to remain at the Casa Santa Maria, the hotel in which he was sequestered along with 114 other cardinals during the conclave that elected him as the Holy Father. The transitory atmosphere of a hotel is perhaps in keeping with the way of life of the former professor of theology.

In Regensburg, Ratzinger rediscovered some of the serenity lost in Tübingen during the turbulence of 1968. It was not in the

character of the man destined to become the prefect of the Congregation for the Doctrine of the Faith to stand aside and passively
observe what he considered a wrongful approach to the teaching
of the Christian tradition. Very soon, together with a group of
friends, he organized a theological counteroffensive.

Communio

Ratzinger's ties to and esteem for his friend Hans Urs von
Balthasar grew stronger in those years, and he considered the
fact that the ideas of his theologian friend had not been shared at
the Council to be a serious loss for the Church. For his part,
Balthasar felt the need to create a way to bring together various per-
sonalities who did not agree with the ideas that had come to dominate the Catholic Church in those years, and that would allow their
thoughts to be heard.

Although they were hardly embarking on a religious war,
their goal was clearly to oppose the ideas that were being spread by
the magazine *Concilium*, which revolved around the thoughts of
Küng. Ratzinger had at first been attracted to the magazine, but
now he saw it as embodying what he, Balthasar, and others felt was
a dangerous deviation from the teachings of Vatican II. They were
concerned that the magazine was seeking to diminish the authority of the Holy See and to propose a vision of the Church that was
more of an "assembly"—a model closer to the ideals of the 1968
protesters than to the two-thousand-year history of the Church.
Both in- and outside the Council, Ratzinger had expressed his
reservations about the Church, but this was not the outcome he had
in mind.

In 1969, at the periphery of the first session of the International Theological Commission, a group of theologian friends laid the foundations for a new magazine. In addition to Balthasar, the soul of the group, and Ratzinger, the best-known name was that of Henri de Lubac, the French Jesuit. Like Balthasar, he would be treated with enormous respect by Pope John Paul II and be nominated as a cardinal on February 2, 1983.

In a speech Ratzinger gave to a conference of Italian bishops in 2002, he explained how this initiative began:

When with a few friends—in particular Henri de Lubac, Hans Urs von Balthasar, Louis Bouyer, Jorge Medina—I had the idea of founding a magazine in which we intended to deepen and develop the inheritance of the Council, we looked for an appropriate name, a single word, which could fully convey the purpose of this publication. Already, in the last year of the Second Vatican Council, 1965, a review was begun, to serve as the permanent voice of the Council and its spirit, called Concilium. *Hans Küng thought he had discovered an equivalence between the words* ekklesia *(Church) and* concilium. *The root of both terms was the Greek word* kalein *(to call), the first word,* ekklesia, *meaning to convoke, the second word,* concilium, *to summon together. Therefore both words essentially signify the same thing. From such an etymological relationship one could say the terms Church and Council were something synonymous and see the Church by her very nature as the continuing Council of God in the world. Therefore, the Church was to be conceived of in this "conciliar" sense and "actualized" in the form of a Council; and, vice versa, the Council was seen as the most intense possible realization of "Church," namely, the Church in her highest form.*

In the years following the Council, for a time, I followed this concept—the Church as the permanent council of God in the world—which seemed at first glance rather enlightening. The practical consequences of this conception should not be overlooked and its attractiveness is immediate. Still, though I came to the conclusion that the vision of Hans Küng certainly contained something true and serious; I also saw that it needed considerable correction.[5]

In an article published in 1992, Ratzinger was even more explicit in explaining Balthasar's view of the trends that were emerging from the post-Vatican II debate. Although the Swiss theologian understood the greatness of the conciliar texts, he was troubled by the way some people were choosing to interpret them:

Their demands corresponded to the taste of their contemporaries and appeared exciting because people had previously assumed that these opinions were irreconcilable with the faith of the Church. Origen once said: "Heretics think more profoundly but not more truly." For the postconciliar period I think that we must modify that statement slightly and say: "Their thinking appears more interesting but at the cost of the truth." What was previously impossible to state was passed off as a continuation of the spirit of the Council. Without having produced anything genuinely new, people could pretend to be interesting at a cheap price. They sold goods from the old liberal flea market as if they were new Catholic theology.[6]

Drawn to the prospect of becoming editors to oppose this mentality, Balthasar, Lubac, Ratzinger, and other friends from the group went to work to create an international magazine, but first they had to address a whole series of problems that were much more material and earthly than the theological matters they intended to discuss in the magazine. Problems such as finding the financing, identifying local publishers that were willing to bring out the magazine in various languages, creating a network of people that would allow them to circulate the magazine in Catholic circles that were more open to their ideas, and convincing authors to join their cause. According to Ratzinger:

> *Two events were decisive for our project to take off. Balthasar contacted the Communion and Liberation movement, which had been established in Italy and was beginning to flourish. The young people that met in the community founded by Father Giussani demonstrated the necessary vitality, willing to take risks, and courageous faith. Thus we had found our Italian partner. In Germany, the Kösel publishing house had decided to drop its traditional culture review,* Hochland, *to replace it with the short-lived* Neues Hochland. *The word "new" referred to a definite change in direction. The last editor of* Hochland, *Franz Greiner, was ready to volunteer his experience and his labor for the magazine. He did so with great generosity and he also founded a publishing house to guarantee the project's independence. Consequently, not only did he refuse any pay for himself, but he also provided his personal means for the whole project. Without him, it would have been impossible to start up the magazine.*[7]

The Italian language edition (brought out by the Jaca Book publishing house) and the German edition were thus assured. One of the major steps the Balthasar group had to take was to choose a name for the magazine. They decided on *Communio*, from the Latin word for communion.

"I can no longer remember exactly how the name *Communio* entered into our conversation at the beginning," recalled Ratzinger, "but I believe that it happened through our contact with Communion and Liberation. The word suddenly appeared, like the illumination of a room. It truly expressed everything that we wanted to say."[8]

The word "communion" was not a large part of the postconciliar vocabulary, which revolved mainly around the concept of the people of God, which was understood in the sense of a popular sovereignty, a right to govern the Church in a democratic way. According to the promoters of *Communio*, God had remained in the discussion, but people had lost the understanding of what it meant that this was His Church. Ultimately, for Ratzinger and the others, what came to prevail in the concept the "people of God," was the people, while God was placed in the back seat.

The word *communio* has an entirely different meaning. It is not a sociological term but rather a theological one. It is related to the Christian concept of communion between God and man, which takes place before the communion of the faithful. On an issue of this type, it is clearly better to rely on the words of Ratzinger for an explanation:

> In the first place, we must remember that "communion" between men and women is only possible when embraced by a third element. In other words, common human nature creates the very possibility that we can communicate with one another. We are not only nature but also persons, and in such a way that each person represents a unique way of being human different

from everyone else. Therefore, nature alone is not sufficient to communicate the inner sensibility of persons. If we want to draw another distinction between individuality and personality, then we could say that individuality divides and being a person opens. Being a person is by nature being related. But why does it open? Because both in its very depths and in its highest aspirations being a person goes beyond its own boundaries toward a greater, universal "something" and even toward a greater, universal "someone." The all-embracing third, to which we return so often, can only bind when it is greater and higher than individuals. On the other hand, the third is itself within each individual because it touches each one from within. Augustine once described this as "higher than my heights, more interior than I am to myself." This third, which in truth is the first, we call God. We touch ourselves in him. Through him and only through him, a communio *which grasps our own depths comes into being.*[9]

Like a Symphony

Today *Communio* is a federation of magazines in seventeen different languages. Its international edition, in English, is published in Washington. D.C., under the direction of David L. Schindler. In his opinion, Catholic debate has too often been reduced to talk of alignments or disagreements between this or that faction. What the magazine proposes instead is a "symphony," made up of the voices of all kinds of authors. This is a concept that is undoubtedly pleasing to Pope Benedict XVI, the great admirer of Mozart.

The list of authors published in recent years suggests that it is a well-tuned orchestra indeed. In addition to Balthasar, Ratzinger, and de Lubac, there is a small group of some of the most highly regarded American Catholic thinkers today, such as Richard John Neuhaus, George Weigel, Michael Novak, Lorenzo Albacete, Carl A. Anderson, and Joseph Fessio. The Italian names include the philosopher-mayor of Venice Massimo Cacciari, the writer Giovanni Testori, Augusto Del Noce, Father Luigi Giussani, and Chiara Lubich. The late American painter William Congdon and the current leader of Communion and Liberation, Julian Carron, were also on the list. Mother Teresa and Aleksandr Solzhenitsyn are two other former contributors.

Communio has proposed or reproposed "pioneers of Catholic renewal," such as Georges Bernanos, Maurice Blondel, G. K. Chesterton, Paul Claudel, Christopher Dawson, Dorothy Day, Madeleine Delbrêl, Etienne Gilson, Charles Péguy, and Josef Pieper, and has dedicated special attention to an author well loved by Ratzinger, Romano Guardini. Particularly noteworthy contributors are a small group of cardinals who participated in the election of Benedict XVI, presumably voting for Ratzinger (the vote and everything else that happens in the conclave is secret): Austrian Christoph Schönborn, Italian Angelo Scola, Frenchman Jean-Marie Lustiger, American J. Francis Stafford, and Canadian Marc Ouellet.

A particularly distinguished byline is that of Karol Wojtyla, John Paul II, who wrote various articles for the magazine, and not only when he was pope. "The founders of the review," said John Paul II in a message to *Communio*, "basing themselves on their intimate encounter with the Lord, knew how to harmonize culture and faith in order to announce the gospel. They united the audacity of creative thought with the most filial and most humble fidelity to the Church and her living tradition."[10]

The editor of the international edition of *Communio*, Schindler, has written:

> *When I learned of the election of Cardinal Ratzinger as Pope, I felt a profound sense of joy. His greatness is visible above all in his humility and simplicity, gifts that fit within the context of an acute intelligence and a great capacity for teaching. People will be surprised by the simplicity and intelligence of Pope Benedict XVI. This man is truly a gift that is being made to the Church. Anyone who describes him as a transitional pope clearly has not known him for twenty years, like I have.* [11]

8. THE ARCHBISHOP

Why I Am in the Church

Heartened to share with a group of theologian friends reservations over the mind-set that had come to dominate the world of Catholic intellectuals, Ratzinger threw himself into a flurry of intense cultural activity. His lectures in Regensburg and work to get *Communio* started were accompanied by conferences and research that kept him in the limelight in theological circles. The sheer quantity of his work impressed his colleagues. The German bishop Engelbert Siebler, who worked with him in the 1970s, recalled that Ratzinger had the habit of dictating "while pacing up and down in the room, and you could then print twenty pages without a single mistake. The way he talked was fit to print."

In 1973, an address that Ratzinger gave to the Bavarian Catholic Academy on the theme, Why am I still in the Church?, had enormous resonance. In it he affirmed the following unequivocally: "Only in the Church is it possible to be Christians and not on the side of the Church."[1] This message was directed, in part, at Küng and the progressive theologians from whom he had broken completely. He continued to meet them in intellectual circles where they

Above: Five-year-old Joseph Ratzinger with his knapsack in Aschau-am-Inn, Germany, 1932.
Left: Joseph Ratzinger (right) and his brother Georg wait with forty-two other men for their ordination to the priesthood in Freising, Germany, June 29, 1951.

Top: An undated family picture of Joseph Sr. and Maria with their children Maria, Georg, and Joseph (right) taken after both sons became priests in the Roman Catholic Church. *Above:* Joseph Ratzinger in 1959, when he was professor of dogma and fundamental theology in the Bavarian village of Freising.

Above: Cologne's
Cardinal Joseph Frings
talking to the young
professor of theology,
Joseph Ratzinger. Frings
brought Ratzinger with
him to the Second
Vatican Council in
Rome as a theological
advisor.
Left: German cardinal
Joseph Ratzinger when
he was a professor
at the University of
Regensburg.

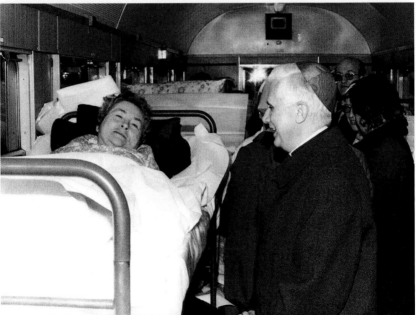

Top: Cardinal Joseph Ratzinger, archbishop of Munich and Freising, acknowledges a
cheering crowd at the marketplace in Munich, July 1, 1977.
Above: Archbishop of Munich and Freising Joseph Ratzinger with handicapped pilgrims
on a train in Munich leaving for Assisi on April 14, 1978.

Top: German cardinal Joseph Ratzinger talks to Pope John Paul II during a cardinals meeting in Rome, November 5, 1979.

Above: Pope John Paul II and Cardinal Joseph Ratzinger pose for photographs with the members of an orchestra in Munich, Germany, November 19, 1980.

Top: Cardinal Joseph Ratzinger walking across Saint Peter's Square, Vatican City, 1983.
Above: Cardinal Joseph Ratzinger inspecting an honor guard of traditionally dressed Bavarian mountaineers during his seventy-fifth birthday celebration, April 20, 2002.

Above: Joseph Ratzinger on the day he became Pope Benedict XVI, April 19, 2005, blessing pilgrims from the balcony of Saint Peter's Basilica at the Vatican.

Left: Pope Benedict XVI walks through the papal apartments in the Vatican, April 20, 2005, with Cardinal Angelo Sodano of Italy and Eduardo Martinez Somalo of Spain. Pope Benedict XVI moved swiftly on the first day of his reign to allay fears of a rigid, authoritarian papacy, saying he would work for dialogue both within the Church and with other faiths.

Top: Pope Benedict XVI greets Metropolitan Kirill of Smolensk, a senior representative of the Russian Orthodox Church, at the Vatican, April 25, 2005. Pope Benedict XVI also met leaders of the Muslim community on that Monday, welcoming progress in Christian–Muslim dialogue and saying the Catholic Church wanted to continue "building bridges of friendship" with all other religions.

Above: Pope Benedict XVI upon his arrival at Rome's Saint Paul's Basilica, his first official visit outside the Vatican City State, April 25, 2005.

debated their scholarly work, and the distance between their approaches was now clear to all.

Years later, Ratzinger explained his concerns about the course that many theologians had taken in the groundbreaking *Ratzinger Report*, a book-length interview with the Italian writer Vittorio Messori. In the book he claimed, "Every theologian now seems to want to be 'creative.' But his proper task is to deepen the common deposit of faith as well as to help in proclaiming it, not 'to create' it." [2]

Ratzinger was bothered by thinkers in the theological world who saw dogma—an ecclesiastical term indicating a definite, indisputable truth—as "an intolerable straitjacket, an assault on the freedom of the individual scholar."

In his opinion, instead, Church dogma should not be seen as bricks in a wall that prevent people from seeing what is outside, but rather as windows that open people's eyes to the infinite. Ratzinger would reprise these themes in his 1973 book, *Dogma and Revelation*, a collection of essays, meditations, and homilies dedicated to the pastoral, and which added to the already considerable bibliography of his works. He was also becoming a successful author. When his previous book, *Introduction to Christianity*, came out in Germany in 1968, it sold fifty thousand copies in a few months; this amazed Ratzinger, who never expected such a response.

Munich and Conclave

Pope Paul VI had kept his eyes on Ratzinger, whom he had met when the young theologian so impressed Vatican II, and during the time when the future pontiff was still known as Cardinal Montini. The papacy of Paul VI dragged on wearily, due to the poor health of the pontiff and the Church's difficulties in communicating its message during the turbulent times of the 1970s, especially in Europe. Pope Paul VI's last encyclical, *Humanae Vitae*, had been written in 1968 and been the subject of so much criticism as to discourage even the pope. It was the document in which for the first time the Church pronounced itself on the subject of artificial contraception, calling it a sin in all its forms and receiving a furious reaction that conveyed the detachment that had been planted between the Vatican's positions and contemporary society.

On March 24, 1977, Paul VI nominated Ratzinger to be the archbishop of Munich and Freising. A Bavarian was to become the pastor of the Bavarians, a momentous event since he was the first priest from that diocese to be chosen for the position in more than eighty years. His ordination as a bishop took place on May 28. Ratzinger's nomination was fast-tracked, assuring that he would become a cardinal quickly. Only one month later, on June 27, 1977, he received the cardinal's cap from the Holy Father in Rome. The "Paul VI" hall was filled to the rafters with Bavarians, who came with him from Munich en masse for the occasion. He had just turned fifty.

Ratzinger did not hide his amazement at how quickly his nomination had gone through. He told the magazine *30 Days*:

> *Two or three days after my episcopal consecration on May 28, I was informed of my nomination as a cardinal, which thus almost coincided with the sacramental ordination. For me it was a great surprise. I still can't explain all this. I do know that Paul VI took notice of my work as a theologian. So much so that some years earlier he had invited me to preach the spiritual exercises in the Vatican. But I didn't feel sufficiently secure either*

of my Italian or of my French to prepare and brave such a ven-
ture, so I declined. But this was proof that the Pope knew me.
Some part in this story might have been played by Monsignor
Karl Rauber, then a close collaborator of the Sostituto,
Giovanni Benelli. Anyway, the fact is, they told me that from the
short list of the nomination for Munich and Freising, the Pope
personally chose my poverty.[3]

For the child who from the age of five had dreamed of becoming a cardinal, not to mention archbishop of his native Bavaria, it
was a dream come true. Besides choosing as his emblem the bear
of Saint Corbinian, a familiar figure to him since his years of study
in Freising, the city where he became a priest, Ratzinger decided on
his motto, which would accompany him in his future decades as a
cardinal: "Collaborators of Truth," a phrase taken from the Third
Letter of John in the New Testament.

From Munich Ratzinger would travel to Rome several times the
next year to meet with the pope, but their collaboration was brief. On
the morning of August 6, 1978, while Ratzinger was on vacation in
Austria, he was informed that the Holy Father was sick and that his
condition was serious. He called the vicar general in Munich and
asked him to invite the whole diocese to pray. On his return from a
short trip to the mountains, Ratzinger learned that the pope had
died. After writing a letter to his diocesans, he left for Rome to attend
the funeral and then to take part in perhaps the most intriguing of the
Catholic Church's ancient rituals: the conclave to elect a new pope.

At the funeral, as Ratzinger told *30 Days*:

I was struck by the absolute simplicity of the coffin with the
Gospels lying on top. This poverty, which the Pope had wanted,

*left me almost stunned. I was also struck at the funeral mass cel-
ebrated by Cardinal Carlo Confalonieri, who would not participate in the conclave since he was over eighty: he gave a beautiful
homily. As was the homily read at another mass by Cardinal
Pericle Felici, who underlined how during the funeral the pages
of the Gospels placed on top of the pope's coffin were rustled by
the wind.* [4]

This description is remarkably similar to that of another
funeral ceremony that would take place almost twenty-seven years
later: the mass for the death of John Paul II, in which it was
Ratzinger's turn to perform the role of celebrant that in 1978 had
been held by Cardinal Confalonieri.

Ratzinger was one of the youngest cardinals in the conclave,
and according to him, he limited himself mainly to listening to others in the discussions leading up to the vote—the informal con-
versations at the dinner table in which alliances were strengthened
and the cardinals got to know the "papabili" a little better. Since he
came from academia, he was less familiar with the ecclesiastical
hierarchies. There are those who say that his role was actually
much more active than he had admitted. He belonged to a small
delegation of German-speaking cardinals that was able to shift
many votes: Joseph Schröffer, former prefect of Catholic Education;
Joseph Höffner of Cologne; the archbishop of Vienna, Franz König;
Alfred Bengsch of Berlin; and two Brazilians of German origin,
Paulo Evaristo Arns and Aloísio Lorscheider.

The man who quickly garnered the majority of votes was
someone Ratzinger had met in 1977 during a mountain vacation
in Bressanone, in the Alto Adige region of Italy: Albino Luciani,
the patriarch of Venice. On August 26, 1978, the second day of the

conclave, the world received the traditional announcement from Saint Peter's: *Habemus Papam*. Luciani appeared to the crowds gathered there and introduced himself as pope with an unusual name: John Paul I.

Ratzinger was very happy about the election of Luciani, because he was a man of great "goodness and a luminous faith." In the weeks that followed, the archbishop of Munich traveled to Ecuador, to celebrate a twinning with the local church. On September 28, 1978, one month after the election of Luciani, devastating news reached him while he was sleeping at the residence of the archbishop of Quito: the new pope was dead. It was time to return to Rome once again, for a new funeral and another conclave, in a Church unsettled by the loss of two leaders in such a short time.

Considerations had to be made not only of a worldly nature but also regarding something much deeper. During a conclave in the Catholic Church, it is believed that it is not only the cardinals who are involved but also the Holy Spirit, who works with them in selecting a pope. So what message was the Holy Spirit sending through the death of a pontificate of only thirty-three days? That a mistake had been made? Or that a turning point had been reached?

After the death of John Paul I, when the cardinals found themselves together again, they started to believe that the second hypothesis was probably right. "Something absolutely new was needed," Ratzinger has said, recalling the thinking of that time.[5]

And something very new was arriving, from the East.

9. FROM MUNICH TO ROME

Pope John Paul II

On October 16, 1978, the cardinals reemerged from the conclave with an extraordinary surprise. The man summoned to appear on the balcony of Saint Peter's Square in the papal vestments was Karol Wojtyla, archbishop of Krakow. The 264th pope of the Catholic Church was the first non-Italian in 455 years and he came from Poland, from that Eastern bloc of communist countries that divided Europe, especially the Germany of Ratzinger, in two. He was an authoritative and brave cardinal who for decades had experienced firsthand the scourge of two totalitarianisms: the Nazis followed by the Communists. He was a refined Catholic intellectual. He was a lover of art, poetry, and theater: a lover of Beauty, in a word.

These were all qualities of a pope that Ratzinger could admire. He himself would often reminisce affectionately about the excitement with which he greeted that moment. In 2003, at a ceremony on the occasion of the twenty-fifth anniversary of the election of John Paul II, Ratzinger told the Holy Father:

Exactly twenty-five years ago, the cardinals who gathered in the
Sistine Chapel elevated you to the office of the successor of Saint

Peter, and you uttered your "yes" to the grace and the weight of that office. Twenty-five years ago the proto-deacon of the Holy College, Cardinal Pericle Felici, announced solemnly to the crowd waiting in Saint Peter's Square, Habemus Papam. *Twenty-five years ago, from the Loggia of Benedictions, you pronounced for the first time the benediction* Urbi et Orbi *and won over instantly, with an unforgettable speech, the hearts of Romans, like the hearts of the many people who followed you and listened to you throughout the world. Then you said that you had come from a distant country. But we immediately sensed that the faith in Jesus Christ that transpired through your words and through your whole person overcame all distances; that in faith we were all close to one another. From the first moment you made us experience the force of Christ, who breaks down borders and creates peace and joy.*[1]

It soon became clear that the esteem between the new pope and the archbishop from Munich was mutual. The new pope had met Ratzinger back in the days of Vatican II, during which the Pole had been appointed to lead the archdiocese of Krakow. Over the years, John Paul II continued to follow with great attention the theological teachings of Ratzinger and his 1977 entry into the ecclesiastical hierarchy, when he was appointed to the prestigious post of archbishop of Munich, the second most important diocese in Germany after Cologne. Once John Paul II became pope, he began almost immediately to try to bring Ratzinger to Rome. As early as 1980, John Paul II wanted him to take over leadership of the Congregation for Catholic Education, but the German cardinal requested and obtained permission to stay in Munich, because he did not want to leave the archdiocese after such a short time.

Although John Paul II reluctantly accepted his reasons, Ratzinger was one of the people he knew he wanted at the Vatican to help him with the colossal undertaking of reanimating a Church that seemed weary after the debates of the 1960s and 1970s, and after the debilitating final years of Paul VI's papacy. John Paul II immediately laid down the foundations of his thinking, in black and white, in his first encyclical, the *Redemptor hominis* of 1979, which revealed the main points of reference for his papacy: "Christ at the center of the cosmos and of history." Then he began to climb aboard airplanes and travel the world, denouncing the situation in his native Poland and encountering massive crowds in every corner of the Earth. Not even the bullets of his would-be assassin in Saint Peter's Square on May 13, 1981, were able to slow him down.

Pope John Paul II was a wellspring of energy, ready to do battle on two fronts: against the totalitarian regimes in Eastern Europe and against the ideologies that undermined the conscience of Western civilization. He needed a theologian like Ratzinger, who could help perfect the ammunition required for a global challenge. But he would have to wait a little while longer.

The Pastor

In Munich Ratzinger found himself as the pastor of a community for the first time. Though more accustomed to life at universities and in cultural circles, he immediately set about to prove that even a man who has spent his life studying theology can lead a complex church system like a diocese. Paul VI's decision to transform a university professor into an archbishop and to send him to a city of one and a half million inhabitants, where the

Catholic community had been led for sixteen years by a cardinal with great charisma and communicative abilities, Julius Dopfner, was a unique and brave gesture. But Ratzinger proved that he was the right man for the job.

From 1977 to the end of 1981, his years in Munich, he was an active bishop on many fronts. The defense of life was one of his key issues. He took public positions on abortion and delivered sermons that stirred great waves and provoked considerable criticism. Drawing on his theological foundations, he tried to translate into simple but content-rich language the comments he had made in previous years about respect for human life, including the unborn. In his view, abortion had become a method of contraception in Germany, and he did not hold back in denouncing the phenomenon, in tones that foreshadowed his future battles as the leader of the Congregation for the Doctrine of the Faith.[2]

Archbishop Ratzinger also took to the streets, in protest marches against what was happening in Poland, where the workers' movement, Solidarity, was coming under increasing attack.

Ecumenical dialogue was another one of his rallying cries, thanks also to his knowledge of Protestant authors and the respect he had for many of them. Since he had taught at universities where Catholics and Protestants had many occasions to converse about theology, he was committed to an ecumenism "without losing one's own identity."

Ratzinger's pastoral activity spread as far afield as Latin America, through a twinning with Ecuador and great fund-raising drives to raise money to send to their communities and to the missionaries working in Latin America.

In addition, a relationship of mutual respect was quickly forged with the local Jewish communities, whose persecution at the hands of the Nazis he knew well. This was fostered by visits to each other's places of worship. He also sought dialogue with non-believers, for whom he organized a series of conferences in which he did not shy away from even the most provocative questions. But one of the most important aspects of his experience as an archbishop was his relationship with young people, whom he gathered together every year by the thousands for the feast of Saint Corbinian. With them he addressed the most difficult issues, explaining patiently the Church's position on the celibacy of priests or on contraception.

This broad array of experiences would come in handy many years later when he was called upon to accept an even higher pastoral assignment.

Becoming Prefect

After the assassination attempt, John Paul II did not waste time returning to work, but in June 1981 he was back at the Gemelli Polyclinic hospital—a place that would become sadly familiar to him in the years to come—for an infection that required surgery. He resumed his active schedule upon release from the hospital; this included the presentation of a new encyclical, *Laborem exercens*, on human labor, at the end of that summer. He also wanted to quickly address an issue of importance: assigning a person that he respected to become leader of one of the most important Vatican departments, the Congregation for the Doctrine of the Faith. Founded in 1542 by Paul III and originally called the Holy Congregation of the Roman and Universal Inquisition (best known as the Inquisition), it is the oldest of the nine congregations of the Roman Curia and one of the longest lasting Vatican institutions. Only the

Secretariat of State, founded in 1487, has older origins. In 1908, Pope Pius X changed the name of the department to the Holy Congregation of the Holy Office and at the end of Vatican II the current name was adopted.

Today the work of the Congregation for the Doctrine of the Faith, which was redefined in 1988 by John Paul II, is to "promulgate and safeguard the doctrine of the faith and practices in the whole Catholic world: therefore everything that in any way touches on this subject falls under its competence." It is not simply a supervisory organization, as it has often been depicted, but also a department that should foster "studies aiming to increase the intelligence of the faith, so that the new problems triggered by the progress of science and civilization can find an answer in the light of faith."

The leader of the Congregation, at the behest of John Paul II, was the Croatian Franjo Seper, who soon asked permission to retire. In 1981, when he had reached the age of seventy-six, his wish was fulfilled by the pope. John Paul once again tried to recruit Ratzinger, and this time the answer was yes (it would have been difficult to say no to the pope twice in the space of less than two years).

The nomination of Ratzinger took place on November 25, 1981, and it was seen as a new step on the road to the implementation of the Council. Never before had the post of prefect gone to a figure of his intellectual stature; instead, it had been the province of men who had made their careers as Vatican insiders, through the ranks of the ecclesiastical hierarchy. Ratzinger went to take his place on the same chair that until the late 1960s had been occupied by the inflexible Roman cardinal Alfredo Ottaviani, who had been the target of much of the criticism that the young theologians at the Council —Ratzinger included—had addressed to the Roman Curia.

In 1968 Ottaviani's place had been taken by Cardinal Seper, who died one month after Ratzinger's arrival in Rome; over the years, the Croatian cardinal had intervened in various postconciliar debates with various types of statements: on the nature of the person of Christ and the infallibility of the Church, on the admission of women to the priesthood, and various issues related to human sexuality. But Seper served primarily under Paul VI. The Church of John Paul II was something new, and the partnership of the pope and Ratzinger promised a different type of challenge to modern thinking and to those who questioned the authority of the Holy See.

10. THE FIRST YEARS IN ROME

The Idea of Freedom

Cardinal Ratzinger arrived in Rome with a personal history and a scholarly focus that had given him a clear and solid vision of the Church's role in the world and how to present the Christian message to people in twentieth century. In an attempt to simplify it as much as possible, with all the attendant risks of inaccuracy that implies, one might say that for him the central idea was that true freedom could be sustained only through the certitude in morals and doctrine. To be truly free one must follow something or someone other than oneself. In the case of the Church, that someone is the Holy Father and the authority of Rome as the continuation of Christ in history.

His studies had given him a serene awareness of these truths. So had the indelible experiences of life. His experience of nazism as a youth, when the Church seemed to be the only solid refuge from Hitler's ideology of death. The "nos filled with goodness" of his father and his mother, which he himself was prepared to pronounce—paternally but forcefully—from the chair of the Congregation for the Doctrine of the Faith. His encounters of 1968 and the consequent attempts to turn the Church into a democratic assembly. The still-open discussion/clash with Communist ideology, which kept Germany split in two and subjugated John Paul II's native Poland.

More than anything else, the greatest risk seemed to come not so much from various political regimes and dictators but from the dominant ideology of society, the expulsion of Christ from daily life, which relegated Him to an occasional appointment at Sunday Mass. To use a word that was at the center of his thoughts at that time, a word that he would repeat on the eve of his election as pontiff, the greatest threat was relativism, "letting oneself be tossed here and there, carried about by every wind of doctrine."

The wealth of statements that his Congregation produced in the quarter of a century that it was led by Ratzinger would require years to study in depth. In these pages we can at best take a quick glance at years of intense activity to defend and promote the faith.

Even before being installed as prefect, Ratzinger already had the opportunity to make a high-level statement in the Vatican on issues that became the focus of his activity in the Congregation for the Doctrine of the Faith. In 1980 he was summoned by John Paul II to be a speaker at the Fifth General Assembly of the Synod of Bishops, dedicated to the theme of the Christian family in the contemporary world: a subject that would remain close to his heart in the years to come. On this occasion he gave a profound talk to inspire and help guide the bishops in their work.

The German cardinal first gave an outline of the condition of the family around the world, depicting an institution under attack by a mind-set that saw it as outdated. To Ratzinger, the role of the woman stood out as fundamental to understanding the meaning and purposes of matrimony. Widening his vision to God's design for the family, he explained that the union of man and woman is not simply a private agreement or a profane or biological question, but rather it is something sacred that changes the status of the couple, introducing them to a new form of permanent, responsible life. Pointing his finger at governments and legislators, he admonished them saying that because of its sacred nature, the family and matrimony somehow take precedence over the public sphere, which must therefore respect them.[1]

Together with his stance on sexuality, which Ratzinger linked directly with fertility, maternity, and procreation, the cardinal's address to the Synod contained the foundation not only for the battle in defense of the family that he undertook in later years, but also the definitive "no" that he would pronounce on closely related issues: contraception, divorce, and same-sex civil unions.

Protector of the Faith

One of the first actions Ratzinger took in his new role as protector of the Catholic faith came in March 1982, when he dampened enthusiasm about a possible reconciliation between the Roman Catholic and the Anglican churches. The idea of a reconciliation was the result of conclusions drawn by an Anglican-Catholic study commission, which had leaked information that was probably interpreted in an overly optimistic way. Ratzinger took paper and pen, wrote a document on the subject, and immediately issued it both to those directly involved in Great Britain and to the international press.

In his note, Ratzinger pointed out that while progress had been made in the dialogue with the Anglicans, serious issues remained on the theme of the Eucharist, the priesthood, and above all, the authority of the Roman Catholic Church. The role of the pope could not be subject to any compromise whatsoever with a religion closely bound to the British monarchy. He wrote: "There are various points held as dogma by the Catholic Church that cannot be accepted as such, or that can be accepted only in part, by our brothers in the Anglican Church." [2]

This encounter revealed the two ways in which Ratzinger intended to administer the prefecture. First of all, he refused to compromise on questions that were central to the Catholic faith. Second, he was going to enlist the media to convey his message, rather than keeping issues locked within the internal debate of the Christian world.

The prefect gave another example of this modus operandi in December 1982, when he convened journalists to a formal press conference and allowed them to question him freely about every possible subject. This was the first time the leader of an important Vatican division had taken an initiative of this type. It was also the fruit of a relationship with the media that had been initiated in those years by the media-savvy John Paul II.

"The Church strives and will strive more and more," the pope told journalists in the early 1980s, "to be a glass house where everyone can see what is happening and how it is fulfilling its mission in fidelity to Christ and to the message of the Gospels." [3]

At a Mass in the Vatican for members of the press, Ratzinger proposed that they compare the figure of Rousseau to that of Saint Francis of Sales, the patron saint of journalists, explaining that Rousseau represented the journalistic world in which criticism was an end in itself, and what counted was "showing that everything is dirty and vulgar," while the saint's message was truth and courage. Ratzinger added, "We certainly need the courage to openly denounce every abuse and to push for improvements, but today more than ever we need the courage to know how to make visible the good in humanity and in the world." [4]

Ratzinger habitually called press conferences to explain his own official documents. He did this, for example, in the very first years of his tenure at the Congregation for the Doctrine of the Faith to illustrate a directive in which he censured some aspects of the activities of various "grassroots" Christian communities, which were multiplying in Europe and Latin America, and which he intended to call to order. Only priests regularly ordained by a bishop could celebrate the Mass, he explained. There was no room in the Catholic Church for free initiatives, women at the altar, or married priests. Whoever moved in that direction, Ratzinger warned, placed himself outside "participation in the unity of the only body of the Lord."

In the years to come he would put these warnings into practice in dealing with a long series of "rebels" who challenged the authority of Rome.

The Ratzinger Report

The best example of Ratzinger's desire to use the media to publicize the Christian message on a global scale was his decision to sit for a long interview that was made into a book. In the interview he explored all the issues on which he intended to work from the helm of the Congregation for the Doctrine of the Faith. It was the summer of 1984. Although Ratzinger had been in Rome for less than three years, he decided to make a bold move with the support of John Paul II. In the attempt to dismantle the stereotype of him as an inquisitor who moved within dark, mysterious rooms of the Vatican, he gave a long interview to the journalist and writer Vittorio Messori (who later became a co-author with the pope). The result was *The Ratzinger Report*, which, for a book of this genre, became an unprecedented international publishing success. It also raised a host of polemics.

Messori related how the project developed in an article that appeared in the Italian newspaper *Corriere della Sera* the day after Ratzinger's election to the papacy. The idea that a prefect of the Congregation for the Doctrine of the Faith would grant a long personal interview—destined, moreover, to become a book—seemed inconceivable to those who had frequented the rooms of the Vatican. Said Messori:

> *And instead the improbable took place. In 1984, a couple of days before Ferragosto [the Italian national holiday on August 15], I pulled my car up into the park of the beautiful seminary of Bressanone, in the Northern Italian Alps, which provided a cheap, no-frills summer vacation to priests and Catholic families. Among the vacationers there was a priest with an intense expression on his face and aristocratic manners, despite his lower-middle-class origins. His hair was already white, his body tiny: a modest clergyman wearing no insignia. This was how the cardinal prefect had spent his two-week annual vacation for years. Out of those few days, he decided to set aside three for me (and I still don't know why). We saw each other in the morning and would converse until lunch, in front of the tape recorder. At the dinner table, the good, corpulent Tyrolese sisters would serve a rustic dish. A short nap and then once again in front of the tape*

recorder. The last two evenings we also saw each other after din-
ner, to revisit and clarify earlier points.[5]

The press release in which the Pauline editions announced the May 1985 release of the book and summarized its contents hinted at its explosive nature: "The first phase after the Second Vatican Council, the phase of confusion and experimentation, is over: for the Church the time of restoration has come, in the sense not of a return backward, but rather of the search for a new balance."

The shock waves it sent were enormous, and it was immediately enmeshed in controversy. At a time when dissenting priests and the grassroots communities spread throughout half the world were enjoying good press, the idea of a "restoration" proposed by one of the pope's top collaborators caused a stir. Messori recounts that he received so many threats he decided to seek refuge in a religious institution for a time. But the book was a huge success around the world. *The Ratzinger Report* became a best-seller and introduced the German cardinal to a larger public.

In the book, Ratzinger reiterated—outside of Catholic intellectual circles—the themes of his clash with the current thinking that, in his opinion, had misinterpreted the Council and wanted to lead the Church down a "catastrophic" path. After a phase of indiscriminate "openness" to the world, claimed Ratzinger, it was time for Christians to regain the awareness that they were a minority and would have to defend what was at the heart of their faith rather than following the trends of the moment or dialogues filled with compromise.

There were raps on the knuckles for everyone, including priests who no longer had an adequate relationship with the sacraments and reduced, for example, the sacrament of confession to a "conversation" with the faithful or to "therapeutic self-analysis between two people at the same level." To Ratzinger, these were all signs of an attempt to follow modernity from a defensive position rather than to take the offense and propose Christ and the millennial traditions of the Church. He criticized the West for its pursuit of economic liberalism, which went arm-in-arm with moral permissiveness, and countered with a defense of the validity of the true Catholic ethic.

The cardinal then focused on issues related to people's personal lives. He criticized the ways in which sexuality was being used, reiterating his rejection of everything that separated the sexual act from the aim of procreation. He also sounded the alarm on the opposite phenomenon, procreation without sex: artificial insemination and the new scientific techniques related to reproduction. There were a few reasons for his admonishments in this area: he wanted to make people aware of the danger of reducing human life to a product, a "thing"; he also was concerned that biological manipulation was being used in the service of man's desire to program everything, including life, disregarding the Mystery.

Homosexuality, abortion, and contraception were once again the subject of warnings aimed not only at society in general, but also at priests and bishops who showed too much openness, in Ratzinger's view, to these themes. Paul VI's encyclical *Humanae vitae*, which had been so harshly criticized, "had not been understood," according to the prefect of the Congregation for the Doctrine of the Faith, but would have to be taken into serious consideration by ecclesiastical circles.

11. THE DISPUTES

Lefebvre

The theologians generally considered progressives are the first to come to mind when one thinks of the acts of censure that Cardinal Ratzinger often took against Catholic intellectuals with whom for years he had been an acquaintance, a colleague, or even a friend. One of his longest and most painful battles as prefect of the Congregation for the Doctrine of the Faith, however, was against an ultraconservative religious reality that was not preaching a leap forward or a revolution in the Church. Instead, it was setting itself up as the guardian of tradition, seeking to erase every innovation that had been introduced by the Second Vatican Ecumenical Council.

The St. Pius X Fraternity was founded in Econe, Switzerland, in 1970 by a French monsignor, Marcel Lefebvre, a bishop who had created problems for the Vatican ever since the times of Pope John XXIII in the early 1960s. Ratzinger inherited the Lefebvre issue from his predecessor. The positions of the ultraorthodox bishop and his followers had already led to drastic consequences.[1] Pope Paul VI had taken direct steps in the mid-1970s, trying to convince

Lefebvre to respect the Vatican's authority once again, but the bishop did not intend to accept any of the directives issued by the Council. In a gesture of open defiance toward the authorities in Rome, Lefebvre ordained three priests on June 29, 1975, violating an explicit prohibition that he had been given. Paul VI had no choice: on July 24, 1976, he decided to suspend him *a divinis*, taking away his right to celebrate the sacraments.[2]

Since then, there had been a long mediation campaign to seek a reconciliation between Rome and the wayward bishop and his followers. Both Paul VI and John Paul II were dedicated to this effort and showed great patience. But it would be up to Ratzinger, from the first years of his arrival at the Vatican, to carry on a dialogue that had been made difficult by Lefebvre's personality and by his vacilations. The situation intensified in 1988.[3] Ratzinger had expressed his willingness to admit back into the fold the followers of the Fraternity, and the previous year he had met with the French bishop. The prefect of the Congregation for the Doctrine of the Faith did not give up his efforts even after Lefebvre's repeated announcements that he intended to appoint bishops, a gesture that would have led to a schism and to his immediate excommunication.

On May 4, 1988, Ratzinger met with Lefebvre at a convent on via Aurelia in Rome, and presented to the wayward bishop a document that had been drafted by theologians from both sides. It was a declaration of submission to the authority of the Pope. Lefebvre said that he wanted his bishops to be nominated by the Pope, but Ratzinger made clear that the decision was entirely up to the Pope and that he had no intention of hurrying the Holy Father.

In the end, the bishop signed the document on May 5, but in a letter of May 6, he announced that he would act on his own behalf and nominate bishops on the following June 29. Ratzinger notified Lefebvre that the consequences would be irreparable, but his warning was not heeded. The bishops were ordained at a ceremony in Switzerland, and from the Vatican the order of excommunication was dispatched immediately.[4]

Lefebvre died in March 1991, without the achievement of any reconciliation with Rome, leaving to his followers the task of deciding on the future of a wayward community that was isolated from the world.

Boff and Liberation Theology

One of the currents that took root in the 1970s in the wake of the postconciliar debate was liberation theology, a phenomenon that become widespread especially in Latin America, but had also extended to other parts of the world, from India to Sri Lanka, the Philippines to Africa.

The basic characteristics of liberation theology was that it interpreted the Christian method through a Marxist lens.[5] The poor, the disinherited, and the needy became the focus of attention for the theologians who were inspired by it. This raised some concerns that religion was becoming too close to left-wing politics. This approach to theology was greatly influenced by the situation in Latin America at that time. In the 1970s and 1980s, the region had become a mosaic of undemocratic governments and regimes, in which representatives of the local Catholic churches, from Mexico to Argentina, had sometimes made dubious compromises with the various dictators and generals.

Ratzinger considered liberation theology particularly insidious because it was the classic phenomenon where, in his view, good, laudable premises led to erroneous conclusions. Christ became the protagonist of the class struggle. The attitude of the Vatican to liberation theology was not wholly negative. John Paul II appreciated its positive aspects and its concern for the needy. His 1987 encyclical, *Sollecitudo rei socialis* (The Social Concern),[6] filled with criticism of the capitalist system, was read by many as an opening to the various theses of South American theologians. Various statements by the ecclesiastical hierarchy in the early 1980s showed an attention to liberation theology that was not necessarily critical.

The main leader of the movement was the Brazilian theologian Leonardo Boff, a Franciscan friar who had been associated with the group revolving around the magazine *Concilium*. Other figures such as Gustavo Gutierrez were considered to have greater intellectual depth, but Boff was the most prominent and well-known of the Latin American theologians, and he also had a talent for using the mass media.[7]

Boff was engaged in a prolonged standoff with Ratzinger. In 1984 he presented himself in Rome to be interrogated for several days by the Congregation for the Doctrine of the Faith. During the same period Ratzinger circulated a document that rejected liberation theology and warned bishops and priests throughout the world to beware of its influence.[8]

On that occasion, Boff experienced firsthand a quality that is a constant in descriptions of Ratzinger by those who have had to answer to him. Ratzinger has never been described as an inquisitor. Sessions with him were almost always more like theological discussions, closer to university exams than to an actual trial. Calm and open to dialogue in his talks with the people he summoned to Rome, Ratzinger became implacable, instead, in his written documents, when he was convinced there were dangers for the Church.[9]

Boff left the Vatican in 1984, convinced that he had somehow gained recognition and approval for his ideas. For a couple of years liberation theology spread without intervention from Rome. But with the passage of time, the Congregation for the Doctrine of the Faith developed strong reservations about the movement and John Paul II shared them. In the ensuing years, the pope nominated a growing number of bishops in Latin America, who did not agree with Boff, Gutierrez, and others.

Slowly but surely, Boff found himself isolated; in the end, he made the decision to leave the Franciscan order and to renounce the religious life. Liberation theology lost steam in the 1990s, until it became a marginal phenomenon; this was also due to the attenuation of many of the political tensions that had torn Latin America apart in the previous decades.[10]

After hearing the news of Ratzinger's election to the papacy, Boff commented ruefully from his house on the outskirts of Rio de Janiero, "The winter of the Church will continue."[11]

Küng and Schillebeeckx

Nothing in Ratzinger's personal history would make it seem as if he would take any special pleasure in exercising his power as prefect. The testimony of his collaborators, for example, describes instead the pain with which, in recent years, he took up the examination of the cases of priests accused of pedophilia, especially in the United States. This was a job for which he set aside time every Friday, which he came to call "our Friday penance."[12]

Among the most difficult cases for Ratzinger to administer were those of theologians with whom he had worked closely during the period of the Council and whom he was now severely reprimanding. The most prominent names were those of Hans Küng and Edward Schillebeeckx.

In 1979, the professor of theology who had once recruited Ratzinger to come to Tübingen, was deprived of the authorization to teach in the name and on behalf of the Catholic Church, after having questioned the foundations of the papal infallibility doctrine.[13] The file on Küng in the archives of the Congregation for the Doctrine of the Faith continued to get fatter with the arrival of Ratzinger.

Schillebeeckx, the Dutch theologian of Belgian origin who had also collaborated with Ratzinger in the past, had been subject to questioning before the German cardinal's appointment to the Vatican.[14] But it was under Ratzinger's watch that he was harshly censured and disciplined. In 1984, Schillebeeckx, a Dominican priest, had circulated theses saying that, in some circumstances, the Eucharist in local communities could also be consecrated by "special ministers": in other words, by non-priests.[15]

The differences between Ratzinger and his former colleagues at *Concilium* was rooted in the past. After Ratzinger's elevation to the papacy, a former colleague at Tübingen, Dietmar Mieth, recalled a lecture that Schillebeeckx had delivered at the university. Küng and Ratzinger were seated next to the podium where the Belgian theologian was questioning the authority of the Church. Küng took the floor after him and described a future in which he imagined the Catholic Church would be reformed. Ratzinger stayed silent. Finally someone from the audience asked for Ratzinger's opinion. "He went to the podium," Mieth related, "and issued a massive critique of what his colleagues had just said. He was indirect. He didn't say that what the others had said was nonsense. He was very informed about the history of theology and the Church, and he provided a lot of quotations that he knew by heart by a lot of people, like Hegel and Schelling and others, to make his point that the position of his colleagues represented a simplification." [16]

Ratzinger had taken his distance from Küng and the others many years earlier. He had also founded the magazine *Communio* to counter their ideas. While he did maintain good personal relations with the dissenting theologians, he had never given an inch on his positions with respect to their ideas. Now that he was the guardian of Catholic orthodoxy, the *Concilium* group saw him as a danger and did not hesitate to attack him openly.

The starting point came with the increasingly harsh criticisms that Ratzinger and John Paul II leveled against liberation theology. On June 25, 1984, Küng and other dissenters published an open letter of defiance to Ratzinger—without naming him—in the *New York Times*; it defended the progressive movements and asked that they be given more room inside the Church. Among the signatories was Küng, Schillebeeckx, the French priest Father J. Phier, Father David Tracey of the University of Chicago, and Father John Coleman of the Theology School of the Jesuits in Berkeley, California. [17]

This dispute led over the years to meetings between the prefect and Küng, at which each refused to budge from his position. Ratzinger took a hard line toward the "wayward" theologians, whom he had considered in error well before his arrival in Rome. He did not grant them authorization to return to teaching with the Church's blessing. He was equally inflexible in judging other rebels through the years, such as the Sri Lankan Tissa Balasuriya, [18] who was excommunicated for supporting women priests and for stating that original sin was an idea cooked up by the clergy "to have power over the souls of the faithful." Another figure with whom he crossed swords was American priest Charles Curran, who had taken controversial stands since the 1960s, when he had strongly criticized the Church's position on contraception and family planning. For years, Ratzinger investigated his teaching and in the end, in 1987, Currant was removed from his chair in moral theology at the Catholic University of America, in Washington, D.C.[19]

The tensions continued for years without resolution. Küng remained substantially outside the Church, without being rehabilitated. Ratzinger had this to say about him in 1997: "I respect the personal path that he has chosen to follow in obedience to his conscience; on his part, however, he cannot expect the seal of approval of the Church, but rather admit to having reached entirely personal decisions of fundamental questions. A new assignment on behalf of the Church would be more senseless now than ever. But none of that matters to Küng: what he would like instead is for his theology to be recognized as an authentic form of Catholic theology."[20]

12. DOMINUS JESUS

From the Masonry to the Catechism

However much attention Ratzinger's focus on orthodoxy may have garnered, it was really only one part of his work leading the Congregation for the Doctrine of the Faith. From the beginning of his tenure, he threw himself into the monumental job of revising varied aspects of life, liturgy, and doctrine, offering explanations, clarifications, documents, and directives. Considering the hard line he took on questions of the faith, positions he shared with John Paul II, his actions were met, more often than not, by indignant reactions from lay people and clergy alike.

This was what happened, for example, when he issued a censure of the Masonry in 1983.[1] Ratzinger reiterated the basic incompatibility between the principles of the Masonic Order and those of the Christian faith, warning Catholics that registration in the Masonic lodges was prohibited by the Church, and that whoever decided to join the world of the Freemasons was committing a "grave sin" and could not receive communion.

On the issue of bioethics, following the stance he took in *The Ratzinger Report*, scientists were repeatedly, forcefully reminded to be respectful of human life and not to consider the human being a product. From cloning to artificial insemination, organ donation, and embryonic research, none of the most sensitive issues on which he debated with scientists escaped his analysis. "That there be values that cannot be manipulated by anyone," he once explained, "is the real, true guarantee of our freedom and of man's greatness; Christian faith sees in this the mystery of the Creator and of the condition of the image of God that He conferred upon man. Now almost no one these days would directly deny the precedence of human dignity and basic human rights over all political decisions; the horrors of nazism and its racist theories are still too recent."[2]

At a Vatican conference in 1996, Ratzinger once again recalled the specter of nazism, relating a rare personal story from his youth in Bavaria. He told an audience of seven thousand people about the time when, at the age of fourteen, he learned that a cousin afflicted by Down's syndrome had been interned in a concentration camp of the Third Reich. Shortly thereafter, the news arrived that his cousin had died "of pneumonia." There was a steady increase in deaths from pneumonia of people with mental disabilities in his Bavarian village, and it quickly became clear that "there was a systematic elimination of anyone who was not considered productive." The State, Ratzinger concluded, had taken upon itself the right to decide who deserved to live and who should be deprived of life. "A new, different kind of shock had been added to the horrors of war. We felt as if the killing of these people humiliated and threatened all of us, the human essence that was in us; if the patience and love that are dedicated to suffering people are eliminated from human life as a waste of time and money, then harm is done not only to the victims, but in such cases the spirit of the survivors is also mutilated."[3]

Here as on other occasions, the cardinal warned people of the "threat of barbarity,"[4] such as nazism. Many times he introduced documents addressed directly to politicians, indicating the positions that should be taken by Catholics engaged in public life.

A major aspect of Ratzinger's work was his collaboration with John Paul II on the drafting of encyclicals or documents on Christian doctrine. He played a key role in the preparation of *Veritatis Splendor* (The splendor of truth), a 1993 encyclical in which John Paul II reiterated the foundations of the Church's moral teaching.[5] A document, the pope stated when he presented it to the faithful, that "reaffirms the dignity and the greatness of the human person, created in the image of God, and reproposes the genuine concept of human freedom, showing the essential, constitutive relationship with the truth, according to the word of Christ: 'The truth shall set you free!'"[6]

A year before the encyclical on morals, Ratzinger had presented the results of one of the major undertakings to which he had dedicated himself since his installation as prefect. It is the work that also preserves one of the greatest legacies left by the papacy of John Paul II: the drafting of a new universal catechism of the Catholic Church.[7]

It took six years of work by a committee chaired by Ratzinger, with the collaboration of thousands of bishops throughout the world, to draft an updated compendium of everything that the Catholic Church believes and how those beliefs are celebrated. Until the beginning of the twentieth century, the Church used for this purpose the catechism of Saint Pius V, which was written in 1566, following the Council of Trent. At the beginning of the twentieth century came the catechism of Saint Pius X. By the end of the century, however, there was a need to rewrite this constitution of the Church in the light of Vatican II and the debate that ensued in the ecclesiastical world. No one could have handled such a task better than Ratzinger the theologian, who had firsthand experience of the Council and spent the years that followed studying its conclusions.

The result was a text more than four hundred pages long that was circulated in every language in every part of the world, and that was also the fruit of the reflections and views of various ecclesiastical movements around the world. Nevertheless, this did not keep Ratzinger, the pope, and the Holy See from once again becoming the target of criticisms for taking too "Roman" an approach to Catholicism. In the world of Western Catholic intellectuals, the reaction was often skeptical and in many cases an outright rejection of the catechism.

Ten years after its presentation, Ratzinger defended the value of the catechism and explained that the moral that characterized it, inspired by Saint Augustine (perhaps his favorite author), was to propose a "doctrine of the fulfilled life, the illustration, so to speak, of the rules to attain happiness."[8]

"The primordial impulse of man, which no one can deny, and which in the ultimate sense no one can oppose," he added, "is the desire for happiness, for a fulfilled, complete life."[9] This is what the Catholic Church was promising in its catechism.

The text of the giant compendium of the Catholic faith has been subject to some changes in the intervening years. The most significant concerns the death penalty. Welcoming signs that had appeared since the publication of the catechism in another papal encyclical, *Evangelium vitae* (The Gospel of life),[10] the cases in which the Catholic Church could accept the death penalty were narrowed significantly. The catechism had left open some possibilities in this regard, which was criticized by the opponents of the death penalty. With the changes announced by Ratzinger, the Catholic Church, in practice, reduced to zero the instances in which it would be acceptable to punish someone by death, in light of John Paul II's belief that the modern state had enough instruments to fight crime as to make recourse to execution inadmissible.

The Christian Claim

It was not easy for Cardinal Ratzinger to overcome the controversies precipitated by *The Ratzinger Report* as well as some of the initiatives that he had taken during his years as prefect of the Congregation for the Doctrine of the Faith. The future pope did score a major success in 2000, the year of the Jubilee, when the Catholic Church saluted the opening of the third millennium since the birth of Christ.

In September of that year, Ratzinger presented a thirty-six-page document entitled *Dominus Jesus* (The Lord Jesus),[11] which could be considered the most important work of his twenty-four years as leader of the Congregation, and definitely an important key to interpreting the papacy of Benedict XVI.

In the document, the Vatican reaffirmed forcefully that the Catholic Church was the only way to the salvation of man. Whatever the merits of other religions, they were to be considered "in a gravely deficient situation" with respect to Catholicism, which underlines the "exclusive and absolute [value] in the history of humanity" of the incarnation of Jesus Christ. Ratzinger's message was that the Church of Rome could not be considered one of many religious options available to man, but rather the only one that leads to the truth and to salvation.[12] To read the Bible outside of the teachings of the Catholic Church, according to the document, was deviant. The dialogue with other religions was reiterated as important and encouraging, but starting from the understanding that the Catholic authority preserved the legacy and the true meaning of the Christian message.[13]

In short, the keys to Paradise were only in Rome.

Ratzinger wrote:

> In the lively contemporary debate on the relationship between Christianity and the other religions, the idea is gaining ground that all religions are for their followers equally valid ways of salvation. This is a widespread persuasion not only in theological circles but also in increasingly large sectors of public opinion, Catholic and non-Catholic, especially those most influenced by the cultural orientation prevalent in the West today, which could be called, without fear of being contradicted, by the word relativism.[14]

He added:

> To believe that there is a universal, binding and valid truth in history itself, that is completed in the figure of Jesus Christ and is transmitted by the faith of the Church, is considered a bit of fundamentalism which is an attack on the modern spirit and a menace to toleration and liberty.

For the cardinal, the true ecumenical dialogue could only be based on the recognition "of the historic figure of Jesus of Nazareth" and on the awareness that the Catholic Church is his direct continuation into history.[15]

Relativism, the danger that Ratzinger also pointed to on the eve of his election as pontiff as the true threat to the contemporary world, was at the center of his reflections at the moment he introduced the document. "The fact that relativism is presented as the true philosophy, able to guarantee toleration and democracy, leads to a further marginalization of those who persevere in the defense of the Christian identity and its claim to spread the universal and salvific truth of Jesus Christ."[16]

There was nothing substantially new about the message of *Dominus Jesus*. It simply reiterated the "Christian claim" that had been at the center of the Church's ideas for two thousand years. Nevertheless, the document was seen as dampening the prospects for the dialogue among religions, and it caused an uproar. Here too, not only the followers of other faiths and lay people were shaking their heads, but also high-level representatives of the ecclesiastical hierarchy.

"If the pope had been ten years younger, a work of this kind would not have been done in this form,"[17] said the aging former archbishop to the Austrian capital, Cardinal Franz Koenig (who would die shortly thereafter). "Salvation is possible for anybody outside of any Church, if each person follows the grace of God, his moral conscience, and the Holy Spirit,"[18] was the response of Cardinal Carlo Maria Martini, archbishop of Milan, one of the most ardent supporters of the dialogue among religions (he was one of the most authoritative of the cardinals gathered for the conclave that elected Ratzinger to the papacy).

Even the head of one of the other departments of the Vatican, Cardinal Edward Cassidy, in charge of interfaith dialogue, distanced himself from the document, claiming that it had been written by someone who was used to always saying, "This is true, this is not true," and was not practiced in dialogue. Cassidy argued that it was an academic document, whose distribution had been ill-timed, and that it did not bear the pope's signature.[19]

Heated criticism arrived from the Jewish and Islamic worlds, which saw the document as a contradiction of the spirit of dialogue among religions promoted by John Paul II, one of the most significant moments of which was the meeting of the world's religious leaders in 1986 in Assisi.

The idea quickly gained ground that the pope, who was already seriously ill and exhausted by the celebrations of the Jubilee, was not entirely in agreement with *Dominus Jesus*. But John Paul II disproved these rumors through one of the surprise gestures that had so often characterized his papacy.

On October 1, 2000, at the end of a ceremony in the Vatican during which 120 Chinese martyrs had been proclaimed saints, the pope suddenly began to talk about Ratzinger's document, explaining that he had wanted and approved "a special form" for it to invite Christians "to renew their faith in Christ." He argued that there was no "arrogance that disdains the other religions" in reiterating the role that Catholics attribute to Jesus Christ.[20]

The pope emphasized that *Dominus Jesus* was a document that he cherished, saying that it had been subject to too many "mistaken interpretations." "Affirming that only in Christ is there salvation," he said, "does not deny salvation to non-Christians." But it had been demonstrated to everybody that the ultimate source of that salvation is Jesus of Nazareth, and the Church believes that it is the way to reach him. A dialogue with others that ignores these basics, the pope concluded, "would be destined to degenerate into empty verbosity."[21]

13. A NEW POPE

The Way of the Cross

Clutching the cross, which for years had been the crutch of his suffering, the pope watched from a television screen the evening procession of the Way of the Cross at the Coliseum in Rome. Dressed in white, with a red stole over his shoulders, he was hunched over, looking worn-out, seated on a chair in his personal chapel in the Apostolic Palace. For the first time since he had become the Holy Father more than a quarter of a century earlier, John Paul II had not been able to be within the midst of the faithful to guide them in the Good Friday ritual. After years of doing battle with a body that could not keep pace with the sharp, active mind it hosted, his health was deteriorating. This time the pope who had never given up would have to resign himself to staying at home in the Vatican.

His image, filmed by an unobtrusive camera, was shown to thousands of people praying at the Coliseum. John Paul II looked at them on television and they looked at the father watching over them. He had not even been able to prepare the meditations for the Stations of the Cross that recalled the Passion of Jesus Christ and his road to Calvary and the crucifixion. The pope had entrusted this task, like so many other things in the recent months, to one of his closest associates, Joseph Ratzinger.[1]

It was the night of March 25, 2005. "I offer my suffering so that God's design may be completed and his word may walk among the people,"[2] said the pope in a message read to the crowd. This would be the last week of his life.

For the most important event of Holy Week, the seven days leading up to the Christian Easter, Ratzinger had offered strong, lacerating reflections. "A Christianity which has grown weary of the faith," he wrote, "has abandoned the Lord: the great ideologies, and the banal existence of those who, no longer believing in anything, simply drift through life, have built a new and worse paganism, which in its attempt to do away with God once and for all have ended up doing away with man. And so man lies fallen in the dust."[3] In what Ratzinger called "the decay of ideologies," Christians had the task of bringing to the world "the new fragrance which returns us to the path of life."[4] Instead, he stated, they were forgetting God.

Nor did he ignore the sins of the Church. Ratzinger asked:

Should we not also think of how much Christ suffers in his own Church? How often is the holy sacrament of his Presence abused, how often must he enter empty and evil hearts! How often do we celebrate only ourselves, without even realizing that he is there! How often is his Word twisted and misused! What little faith is present behind so many theories, so many empty words! How much filth there is in the Church, and even among those who, in the priesthood, ought to belong entirely to him! How much pride, how much self-complacency! What little respect we pay to the Sacrament of Reconciliation, where he waits for us, ready to raise us up whenever we fall![5]

These words shook the consciences of his listeners. The pope was listening to them in his chapel, clutching the cross, unable to speak. Now it was Ratzinger who was speaking for him, who had become the spokesperson for the anxiety with which John Paul II was preparing to leave the Church.

The early months of 2005 were a period of enormous grief for Catholics. But few were called upon to carry the weight that fell on Ratzinger's shoulders. The pope's deteriorating health and his consequent hospitalizations forced a small group of his closest confidantes, including the prefect of the Congregation for the Doctrine of the Faith, to hold the reins of the Church and begin to think, sadly, of the future.

For Ratzinger, it was a time of saying farewell to good friends. On February 24, the cardinal traveled to the Milan Cathedral to preside over the funeral Mass for Father Giussani, the founder of Communion and Liberation (CL), the movement that ever since the first steps of *Communio* had established a special dialogue with Ratzinger. The CL congregation at that Mass was the first of the many large gatherings the cardinal would address in the following weeks. Before tens of thousands of people, he painted a picture of the departed priest. Mixed in with his many reminiscences and comments on Father Giussani's charisma, Ratzinger mentioned one quality that he must have particularly cherished: "Father Giussani grew up in a home—as he himself said—poor as far as bread was concerned but rich with music, and thus from the start he was touched, or better wounded, by the desire for beauty. He was not satisfied with any beauty whatsoever, a banal beauty: he was looking rather for Beauty itself, infinite Beauty, and thus he found Christ, in Christ true beauty, the path of life, true joy."[6] For the cardinal who was a lover of music, who could be deeply moved by listening to a symphony, that attribute contained something familiar, something that recalled his own childhood in Bavaria.

The Milan ceremony took place at the same time as the pope was being treated at the Gemelli Polyclinic in Rome. A few days later, on March 1, Ratzinger went to see him in the hospital, and later mentioned that he found the Holy Father lucid, and that they had conversed in German and Italian. In the weeks that followed, however, the situation would worsen.

The Farewell to John Paul "the Great"

Holy Week was yet another occasion for the world to realize that Pope John Paul II's death was imminent. One after the other, he was forced to cancel his most important appointments. Recovering from surgery, a tracheotomy, John Paul II not only entrusted the meditations for the Stations of the Cross to Ratzinger but also the celebration of the Mass for the Easter Vigil. "Let us awaken from our weary, listless Christianity," he said.[7]

As a result of the pope's deteriorating health, the worldwide media descended on Saint Peter's Square in the coming days. Pilgrims arrived by the thousands; each person who passed cast his gaze upward to the window of the papal apartment.

Ratzinger was one of those who remained by the Holy Father's side to the end. On the evening of April 1, the day before the pontiff's death, Ratzinger took a brief trip outside of Rome, to Subiaco, for a conference that had long been scheduled and that assumed the status of prophecy. Subiaco is the location of the medieval Benedictine Abbey of Saint Scholastica, Saint Benedict's sister. In this place so replete with history and reminders of the saint, Ratzinger spoke at length about Europe and the crisis of cultures, pointing to the example left by Benedict of Norcia. Said the cardinal who would adopt the name Benedict less than one month later:

What we truly need in this moment of history are men who, through an illuminated, living faith, make God credible in this world. The negative witness of Christians who speak of God and live against Him, has obscured the image of God and opened the door to incredulity. We need men who keep their eyes straight on God, and thus learn true humanity. We need men whose intellect is illuminated by the light of God and to whom God opens his heart, in such a way that their intellect can speak to the intellect of others and their hearts can open to others. Only through men that have been touched by God can God return among men.

He continued:

We need men like Benedict of Norcia, who in a time of dissipation and decadence, plunged himself into the most extreme solitude, succeeding, after all the purifications to which he would submit, in climbing back to the light, to return to and found Montecassino, the city on the mountain that, from so many ruins, put together the forces from which a new world is formed. And so Benedict, like Abraham before him, became the father of many populations.[8]

Ratzinger returned to Rome, accompanied by the Benedictine inspiration.

The pope passed away on Saturday, April 2; the pope who had wanted him in the Vatican and never again allowed him to leave.

The people's response to the death of John Paul II exceeded expectations. Hundreds of thousands and then millions lined up to pay homage to the body of the pontiff lying in state. The most powerful leaders of the world came to Rome for the most important funeral in memory. The pope's death dominated television news coverage throughout the world. The Church hastened to call John Paul II "the Great." In the days that followed, the people began to demand something more. *Santo subito!* (make him a saint right away)was the cry that rose from the Square.

To the prefect of the Congregation for the Doctrine of the Faith fell the task, as dean of the College of Cardinals that would elect the new pope, of administering the complex ceremonies of the days of mourning as well as the conclave.

Ratzinger, who had been known to the larger public before this moment primarily as the inflexible custodian of Vatican tradition, surprised people with the simplicity and affection of his funeral homily: "We can be sure that our beloved pope is now at the window of the Father's house, he sees us and blesses us. Yes, bless us, Holy Father. We entrust your dear soul to the Mother of God, to your Mother, who has guided you every day and will now guide you to the eternal glory of His Son, Jesus Christ our Lord."[9]

The cardinals, their vestments fluttering in the wind—which was also flipping the pages of the Gospels resting on the simple wooden coffin of John Paul II—listened to Ratzinger and perhaps began to see him as the man to whom the future of the Church should be entrusted. Among the heads of state and government leaders present in Saint Peter's Square, his homily was greatly admired.

Aboard Air Force One, on his way back to the United States from Rome, President George W. Bush stopped to praise Ratzinger's speech, telling the journalists that the ceremony had

been, "one of the highlights of my presidency." "I thought the homily was really good," said Bush. "We were given an English version,
fortunately—if you haven't read it, maybe you've seen it? Yes. Beautiful. Beautiful. Beautifully done."[10]

As the days went by, Ratzinger showed that he knew how to
find the right tone, and to mix his reminiscences of the departed
Holy Father with warning against the risks that persisted in the
world that John Paul II left behind. First and foremost was relativism. Also at his last public mass on the morning of April 18, the
day on which 115 cardinals were about to retire into the conclave in
the Sistine Chapel to choose the new pope, Ratzinger did not limit
himself to a homily referring only to the present circumstances.
Instead, he gave a summary of the dangers emerging in contemporary society that he had been striving for years to point out and
correct as the prefect of the Congregation for the Doctrine of the
Faith. He did not conclude on a note of pessimism, however, but
rather by pointing to the task of the future:

> We have a different goal: the Son of God, true man. He is the meas-
> ure of true humanism. Being an "Adult" means having a faith
> which does not follow the waves of today's fashions or the latest
> novelties. A faith which is deeply rooted in friendship with Christ
> is adult and mature. It is this friendship which opens us up to all
> that is good and gives us the knowledge to judge true from false,
> and deceit from truth. We must become mature in this adult faith;
> we must guide the flock of Christ to this faith. And it is this faith—
> only faith—which creates unity and takes form in love.[11]

From here on in the question seemed to have been settled for
the cardinals. It made no sense to continue the search. Ratzinger

was the right pastor for the assignment, at this historic moment, of the flock of the Catholic Church.

Twenty-four hours after the start of the conclave, the smoke from the chimney on the roof of the Sistine Chapel turned from black to white. After the mourning of the previous days, the bells of Rome began to toll in celebration.

Pope Benedict XVI

Rushing toward Saint Peter's from the other side of the Tiber River, swarming from office buildings, huffing and puffing in jackets and ties, in dresses and high heels, wearing workmen's suits, uniforms, and jeans and sneakers, hundreds of thousands of people began to stream into the Square in a few short minutes, until it was jam-packed.

Habemus Papam!—We have a pope!—was the annunciation from the balcony of the basilica. And then Ratzinger appeared, this time with a name borrowed from a pacifist pope of the early twentieth century and from the saint that had saved Western civilization.

"After the great pope John Paul II," was his first message, "the cardinals have elected me, a simple worker in the vineyard of the Lord."[12]

The boy who had dreamed of becoming a cardinal, the brilliant young theologian who forty-three years earlier had amazed the entire Vatican with his knowledge, the guardian of the faith who did not fear being unpopular in his defense of the heart of Christianity, had now become the new successor of Peter. A responsibility that he accepted with fear and nervousness, but also with obedience.

"I prayed to the Lord to choose someone stronger," Pope Benedict XVI confessed to a group of German pilgrims a few days after his election, "but evidently he did not listen to me. The ways of the Lord are not comfortable, but we are not made to be comfortable."[13]

He had immediately rejected the temptation to be afraid. To his flock, to young people, to the world, Benedict XVI appeared at the Mass of his papal installation with an inaugural message that rejected a timorous approach to Christianity, and offered an alternative:

> *At this point, my mind goes back to October 22, 1978, when Pope John Paul II began his ministry here in Saint Peter's Square. His words on that occasion constantly echo in my ears: "Do not be afraid! Open wide the doors for Christ!" The Pope was addressing the mighty, the powerful of this world, who feared that Christ might take away something of their power if they were to let him in, if they were to allow the faith to be free. Yes, he would certainly have taken something away from them: the dominion of corruption, the manipulation of law, and the freedom to do as they pleased. But he would not have taken away anything that pertains to human freedom or dignity, or to the building of a just society. The Pope was also speaking to everyone, especially the young. Are we not perhaps all afraid in some way? If we let Christ enter fully into our lives, if we open ourselves totally to him, are we not afraid that He might take something away from us? Are we not perhaps afraid to give up something significant, something unique, something that makes life so beautiful? Do we not then risk ending up diminished and deprived of our freedom? And once again the Pope said: No! If we let Christ into our lives,*

we lose nothing, nothing, absolutely nothing of what makes life free, beautiful, and great. No! Only in this friendship are the doors of life opened wide. Only in this friendship is the great potential of human existence truly revealed. Only in this friendship do we experience beauty and liberation. And so, today, with great strength and great conviction, on the basis of long personal experience of life, I say to you, dear young people: Do not be afraid of Christ! He takes nothing away, and he gives you everything. When we give ourselves to him, we receive a hundredfold in return. Yes, open, open wide the doors to Christ—and you will find true life.[14]

THE LIFE OF BENEDICT XVI:
A CHRONOLOGY

1927: Joseph Alois Ratzinger was born on April 16, Holy Saturday, at a house on 11 Marktplatz in Marktl-am-Inn, in Bavaria (Germany). The son of a policeman, Joseph Sr., and a former hotel cook, Maria, he is the third and last child, after Georg and Maria.

1929: The Ratzingers move to Tittmoning, near the Austrian border.

1932: The family moves again, this time to Aschau-am-Inn, near the Alps.

1937: The family settles in Traunstein, the Bavarian town where Joseph spends most of his teenage years. He begins his studies at the local school.

1939: Joseph Ratzinger enters the minor seminary of Saint Michael.

1943: He receives an order to appear on August 2 to join the German military. He is initially assigned to the Flak, the anti-aircraft artillery, near Munich. He is then sent to install anti-tank traps near the Austrian border.

1945: Having reached the age of eighteen, he is ordered to undergo formal military training in the infantry. Between April and May he decides to desert. He returns to Traunstein and is taken prisoner by the Americans when they arrive in the city. He is a prisoner for several weeks, and later returns home. The war is over. In November he and his brother Georg resume their studies.

1947: He transfers to the Georgianum seminary in Munich, continuing his studies at the Higher School of Philosophy and Theology of Freising.

1951: Joseph and Georg Ratzinger are ordained priests on June 29 in Freising by Cardinal Faulhaber.

1953: Joseph receives his doctorate in theology from the University of Munich. Over the course of four years he presents two major works, one on Saint Augustine, the other on Saint Bonaventure.

1959: He moves to Bonn, where he teaches fundamental theology until 1963. On August 23 his father dies.

1962: He participates as the "expert" of the archbishop of Cologne in the Second Vatican Ecumenical Council in Rome and distinguishes himself. He becomes one of the most highly regarded theologians of the younger generation.

1963: He takes a post as professor of theology at the University of Münster (Germany). On December 16 his mother, Maria, passes away.

1966: With the support of the theologian Hans Küng, he transfers to the University of Tübingen (Germany).

1968: He publishes *Introduction to Christianity*, the first work to make him well-known outside of scholarly circles.

1969: He leaves Tübingen because of the climate created by the student protests and the positions taken by his fellow teachers. He transfers to the University of Regensburg (Germany), in Bavaria.

1972: Together with the theologians Hans Urs von Balthasar and Henri de Lubac, he founds the magazine *Communio*, which appears initially in Italian and German, and then in other languages. The magazine firmly opposes the ideas of the group gravitating around Küng and their magazine, *Concilium*.

1977: On March 24, Pope Paul VI nominates him to be archbishop of Munich and Freising. His ordination as bishop comes on May 28. On June 27 he is nominated cardinal.

1978: On August 6 Pope Paul VI dies. Ratzinger travels to Rome for the conclave that, on August 26, elects as pope patriarch of Venice Albino Luciani, who takes the name John Paul I. On September 28 Pope Luciani dies. Ratzinger returns to Rome for a new conclave. On October 16, the archbishop of Krakow is elected, taking the name John Paul II.

1981: On November 25, John Paul II appoints him as prefect of the Congregation for the Doctrine of the Faith.

1985: He publishes his book-length interview, *The Ratzinger Report*, which becomes an international best-seller.

1992: He introduces the new edition of the Universal Catechism of the Catholic Church.

2000: He introduces the document *Dominus Jesus*.

2005: He prepares the meditations for the Way of the Cross, taking the place of the ailing pope. John Paul II dies on April 2. As dean of the College of Cardinals, Ratzinger presides over the funeral rites, delivers the homily at the funeral in Saint Peter's Square, and leads the cardinals in the election in the Sistine Chapel. On April 19 he is elected as the 265th pope in history. He chooses the name Benedict XVI.

IN HIS OWN WORDS

Below is a collection of excerpts from public statements made over the years by Cardinal Joseph Ratzinger, from texts that he penned as prefect of the Congregation for the Doctrine of the Faith, as well as from his first statements as Pope Benedict XVI.

September 11 (2002)

It is important not to simply attribute what happened on September 11, 2001, to Islam. It would be a great error. While it is true that in the history of Islam there is also a tendency toward violence, there are also other aspects: a true reality of opening to the will of God. It is thus important to contribute to the prevalence of the positive orientation in the Islamic world, an orientation that exists in its history and that is strong enough to prevail over the other orientation.

International Days of Philosophical Thought Conference in Trieste, Italy, September 20, 2002 (from Avvenire and ANSA Italian News Agency)

Abortion (1987)

Any legalization of abortion implies the idea that force is what founds law and thus, mostly unawares, the very foundations of any authentic democracy, based on the justice system, are undermined. (. . .) People thus become blind to the right to life of the other, of the small and the weak, of the voiceless. The rights of others should not be affirmed by the loss of the fundamental right to life of another person.

The Right to Life and Europe Conference, Aula Magna Augustinianum, Rome, December 19, 1987 (from *L'Osservatore Romano*)

Beethoven, the Ninth Symphony, and the Hymn to Joy (2003)

One of the great musical masterpieces, Beethoven's Ninth Symphony, echoes the inner strife of the great maestro in the midst of the darkness of life, his passage, as it were, through dark nights in which none of the promised stars seemed any longer to shine in the heavens. But in the end, the clouds lift. The great drama of human existence that unfolds in the music is transformed into a hymn of joy for which Beethoven borrowed the words of Schiller, whose true greatness blossomed only through his music . . . Compared with the intact presence of the faith that transpires in Handel's *Hymn to Joy* and which emerges in a very different way, that is, as a tranquil inner peace and the grace of reconciliation, in Bach's *Christmas Oratorio* or at the end of his *Passions*, the illuminating Ode by Schiller, so impressively set to music by Beethoven, is characterized by the humanism of that time, which places man at the center and—where there is a reference to God—prefers the language of myth. Nevertheless, we should not forget that Beethoven is also the composer of the *Missa Solemnis*. The good Father, of which the Ode speaks, is not so much a supposition, as Schiller's text might suggest, but rather, an ultimate certainty. Beethoven also knew that we can entrust ourselves to the Father because in the Son he made himself close to us. And thus, we can calmly see the divine spark, of whose joy the Ode speaks, as that spark of God which is communicated to us through the music and reassures us: yes, the good Father truly exists and is not utterly remote, far beyond the firmament, but thanks to the Son is here in our midst.

Spoken at concert by the Mitteldeutscher Rundfunk Orchestra, Vatican City, December 17, 2003, celebrating the twenty-fifth anniversary of the pontificate of John Paul II

Beauty (2002)

Is there anyone who does not know Dostoyevsky's often quoted sentence: "The Beautiful will save us?" However, people usually forget that Dostoyevsky is referring here to the redeeming Beauty of Christ. We must learn to see Him. If we know Him, not only in words, but if we are struck by the arrow of his paradoxical beauty, then we will truly know him, and know him not only because we have heard others speak about him. Then we will have found the beauty of Truth, of the Truth that redeems. Nothing can bring us into close contact with the beauty of Christ himself other than the world of beauty created by faith and light that shines out from the faces of the saints, through whom his own light becomes visible.

The Feeling of Things, the Contemplation of Beauty, message to the Communion and Liberation (CL) meeting at Rimini, August 24–30, 2002 (from *30 Days*, September 2002)

Catholics and Politics.
Freedom and Truth (2003)

Christian faith has never presumed to impose a rigid framework on social and political questions, conscious that the historical dimension requires men and women to live in imperfect situations, which are also susceptible to rapid change. For this reason, Christians must reject political positions and activities inspired by a utopian perspective which, turning the tradition of Biblical faith into a kind of prophetic vision without God, makes ill use of religion by directing consciences toward a hope which is merely earthly and which empties or reinterprets the Christian striving toward eternal life.

At the same time, the Church teaches that authentic freedom does not exist without the truth. "Truth and freedom either go together hand in hand or together they perish in misery." [John Paul II, *Fides et ratio*] In a society in which truth is neither mentioned nor sought, every form of authentic exercise of freedom will be weakened, opening the way to libertine and individualistic distortions and undermining the protection of the good of the human person and of the entire society.

Doctrinal Note on some questions regarding the participation of Catholics in political life, Vatican City, November 24, 2002 (from *Traces*, March 2003)

Cloning (1997)

To fabricate man and make him a product of our chemical arts or any other technology is a fundamental attack on the dignity of man, who is no longer considered, no longer realized as an immediate creature of God and his immortal vocation. . . . It is essential to respect the unique dignity of man, who is wanted and created immediately by God, always through a new miracle of creation. [Through cloning, the human person] becomes our product, a product of our art: thus his dignity as a human person is violated from the start.

Vatican Radio, interview with Cardinal Ratzinger (from ANSA, March 7, 1997)

Crisis of Cultures (2005)

The true contrariety that characterizes the world of today is not among diverse religious cultures, but rather between the radical emancipation of man from God, from the roots of life, on the one hand, and the great religious cultures on the other. If a conflict of cultures occurs, it will not be through a conflict of the great religions—forever one against the others, but, ultimately always able to coexist—but rather through the conflict between this radical emancipation of man and the great historic cultures.

Conference held on April 1, 2005, at the Saint Scholastica Monastery, Subiaco

Christians and Ecumenicism (2005)

With full awareness, therefore, at the beginning of his ministry in the Church of Rome which Peter bathed in his blood, Peter's current Successor takes on as his primary task the duty to work tirelessly to rebuild the full and visible unity of all Christ's followers. This is his ambition, his impelling duty. He is aware that good intentions do not suffice for this. Concrete gestures that enter hearts and stir consciences are essential, inspiring in everyone that inner conversion that is the prerequisite for all ecumenical progress.

Theological dialogue is necessary; the investigation of the

historical reasons for the decisions made in the past is also indispensable. But what is most urgently needed is that "purification" of memory, so often recalled by John Paul II, which alone can dispose souls to accept the full truth of Christ. Each one of us must come before him, the supreme Judge of every living person, and render an account to him of all we have done or have failed to do to further the great good of the full and visible unity of all his disciples.

The current Successor of Peter is allowing himself to be called in the first person by this requirement and is prepared to do everything in his power to promote the fundamental cause of ecumenism. Following the example of his Predecessors, he is fully determined to encourage every initiative that seems appropriate for promoting contacts and understanding with the representatives of the different Churches and Ecclesial Communities. Indeed, on this occasion he sends them his most cordial greeting in Christ, the one Lord of us all.

First message of His Holiness Benedict XVI at the end of the Eucharistic Concelebration with the members of the College of Cardinals in the Sistine Chapel, April 20, 2005 (VIS—Vatican Information Service)

Enlightenment Culture (2005)

The reasons for this "no" [to the insertion of a reference to God in the European constitution and to the mention of the Judeo-Christian roots of Europe] are much deeper than one would imagine from the reasons that have been given. They presuppose the idea that only enlightenment culture, which attained its full development in our times, could be constitutive of European identity. Therefore the different religious cultures with their respective rights can only coexist alongside it, on the condition and to the measure that they respect and are subordinate to the criteria of enlightenment culture. Enlightenment culture is substantially defined by the rights to freedom; it assumes that freedom is the fundamental value that measures all: freedom of religious choice, which includes the religious neutrality of the State; the freedom to express one's own opinion, on the condition that it does not question this canon; the democratic order of the State, namely parliamentary control over government bodies; the free formation of political parties; an independent judiciary; and finally the safeguarding of human rights and the prohibition of discrimination. Here the canon is still being formed, since there are also contradictory human rights, such as the case of the contrast between a woman's desire for freedom and the right to life of the unborn. The concept of discrimination is broadened more and more, so that the ban on discrimination can be increasingly transformed into a restraint on opinion and religious freedom. Soon it will no longer be possible to affirm that homosexuality, as the Catholic Church teaches, constitutes an objective disorder in the structure of human existence. And the fact that the Church is convinced that it does not have the right to ordain women as priests has by some been considered, thus far, irreconcilable with the spirit of the European Constitution. Clearly this canon of enlightenment culture, which is hardly final, contains values that are important for us, and as Christians we do not and cannot be without it; but it is equally clear that the poorly defined or even undefined concept of freedom at the basis of this culture inevitably leads to contradictions; and it is clear that precisely because of its use (a use that seems radical) it entails restraints on freedom that one generation ago we could not even imagine. A confused ideology of freedom leads to a dogmatism that is proving increasingly hostile to freedom.

Conference held on April 1, 2005, at the Saint Scholastica Monastery, Subiaco

The Destiny of Europe (2004)

Europe, precisely in this its hour of maximum success, seems to have become empty inside, paralyzed in a certain sense by a crisis in its circulatory system, a crisis that puts its life at risk, resorting, as it were, to transplants that cannot but eliminate its identity. To this interior failure of its fundamental spiritual powers corresponds the fact that, even ethnically, Europe appears to be on the way out.

There is a strange lack of desire for a future. Children, who are the future, are seen as a threat for the present; the idea is that they take something away from our life. They are not felt as a hope, but rather as a limitation of the present. We are forced to make comparisons with the Roman Empire at the time of its decline: it still worked as a great historical framework, but in practice it was already living off those who would dissolve it, since it had no more vital energy.

Lectio magistralis on "The Spiritual Roots of Europe," Sala Capitolare, Monastery of Santa Maria sopra Minerva, Rome, May 13, 2004 (Archive of the Italian Senate)

Families, Domestic Partners, Gays (2004)

We all know how threatened marriage and the family are at present—on one hand by eroding their indissolubility through easier forms of divorce, and on the other hand by means of a new and more and more widespread lifestyle, the cohabitation of man and woman without the juridical form of marriage. In stark contrast to all this is the request for communion of life between homosexuals, who paradoxically now demand a juridical form having the same value as marriage. This tendency marks a departure from the system of mankind's moral history, which, notwithstanding all the diverse juridical forms of marriage, always recognized that marriage is, in its essence, the particular communion of man and woman that is open to children and thus to the family. This is not a question of discrimination, but rather the question of what the human person is, as man and woman, and of how the togetherness of man and woman can be given a juridical form. If on one hand their togetherness is more and more detached from juridical forms, and on the other hand, homosexual union is seen more and more as having the same value as marriage, then we are before a dissolution of man's image that can have only extremely grave consequences.

Lectio magistralis on "The Spiritual Roots of Europe," Sala Capitolare, Monastery of Santa Maria sopra Minerva, Rome, May 13, 2004 (Archive of the Italian Senate)

Faith (1993)

Faith is the heart's obedience to the form of teaching to which we have been consigned.

Conference of Cardinal Ratzinger in Florence, Italy

The Historic Figure of Jesus (2001)

The problem central to our time is the emptying of the historic figure of Jesus Christ. An impoverished Jesus cannot be the sole Savior and Mediator, the God-with-us; thus, Jesus is substituted with the idea of the "values of the kingdom," and becomes a vain hope. We must go back clearly to the Jesus of the Gospels, because he alone is the true historic Jesus.

Tenth Synod of Bishops, October 6, 2001

Fundamentalism and
Religious Indifference (2002)

There are different forms of fundamentalism. For example, the U.S. bishops prefer not to use the word fundamentalism to indicate violent extremism, because part of the Protestant world in the United States describes itself as fundamentalist, but without falling prey to violence and fanaticism.

And religious indifference also has different forms. There are those who do not regard themselves as Christian but who have an underlying ethical impulse. And there is also the anarchic and arrogant indifference of those who presume to dismantle man and remake his pieces in their way and not according to the logic of the Creator.

Zenit News Agency, Cardinal Ratzinger highlights Christian challenge following Sept. 11 "We See More Clearly the Abyss Man Faces," Lugano, Switzerland, March 3, 2002

John Paul II (2005—Funeral Mass)

The Holy Father found the purest reflection of God's mercy in the Mother of God. He, who at an early age had lost his own mother, loved his divine mother all the more. He heard the words of the crucified Lord as addressed personally to him: "Behold your Mother." And so he did as the beloved disciple did: "He took her into his own home" (John 19:27)—"Totus tuus." And from the Mother he learned to conform himself to Christ.

None of us can ever forget how in that last Easter Sunday of his life, the Holy Father, marked by suffering, came once more to the window of the Apostolic Palace and one last time gave his blessing *urbi et orbi*. We can be sure that our beloved Pope is standing today at the window of the Father's house, that he sees us and blesses us.

Yes, bless us, Holy Father. We entrust your dear soul to the Mother of God, your Mother, who guided you each day and who will guide you now to the eternal glory of her Son, our Lord Jesus Christ.

Justifiable War 1 (2001)

Justifiable war is defined on the basis of these parameters: 1–It is truly the only possibility for defending human life, defending human values; has the whole situation been pondered truly in the conscience and have other alternatives been pondered? 2–That only the immediate means needed for this defense are used and that law is respected; in such a war, the enemy would have to be respected by man and all his fundamental rights would have to be respected. The responses of the Christian tradition have to be updated on the basis of the new possibilities of destruction, the new threats. They should thus be updated, but I would say that you cannot totally exclude a priori any need, including moral, to defend people and values through proper means, against unjust aggressors.

Vatican Radio, interview with Cardinal Ratzinger (from ANSA, November 13, 2001)

Justifiable War 2 (2004)

This is a great problem. When there is an aggression by an evil that threatens to destroy not only values and people but also the very image of man, to defend oneself, also to defend others, can be a duty. The father of a family who sees his children assaulted has the duty to do everything possible to defend his family, also through the possibility of appropriate violence.

Vatican Radio, interview with Cardinal Ratzinger (from ANSA, April 19, 2004)

Preventive War (2002)

The concept of preventive war does not appear in the Catechism. One cannot simply say that the Catechism does not legitimate war, but it's true that the Catechism has developed a doctrine such that, on the one hand, there may be values and populations to defend in certain circumstances, but on the other, it proposes a very precise doctrine on the limits of these possibilities.

International Days of Philosophic Thought Conference in Trieste, Italy (from *Avvenire*, September 21, 2002)

Incarnation (1997)

The incarnation is not an ordinary philosophic principle, according to which the spiritual should always become flesh and express itself in correspondence with various situations. The incarnation is not a philosophical idea but a historic event, which precisely in its unique nature and truth is the point at which God enters history and at which we encounter him. If you consider it, as the Bible demands, not as a principle but as an event, then the consequence is the exact opposite: God has associated himself with a specific historic point with all its limitations and wants his humility to become ours.

The Eucharist as Genesis of the Mission, Eucharistic Congress (from *Traces*, October 1, 1997)

Islam and the West (2004)

The rebirth of Islam is due in part to the new material richness acquired by Muslim countries, but mainly to the knowledge that it is able to offer a valid spiritual foundation for the life of its people, a foundation that seems to have escaped from the hands of old Europe, which has thus, despite its lasting political and economic power, come to be seen increasingly as condemned to decline and fall.

Lectio magistralis on "The Spiritual Roots of Europe," Sala Capitolare, Monastery of Santa Maria sopra Minerva, Rome, May 13, 2004 (Archive of the Italian Senate)

Freedom (2005)

Freedom, in order to be true, human freedom, freedom in truth, needs communion. An isolated freedom, a freedom only for the "I," would be a lie, and would destroy human communion. In order to be true, and therefore in order to be efficient, freedom needs communion, and not just any kind of communion, but ultimately communion with truth itself, with love itself, with Christ, with the Trinitarian God. Thus is built community that creates freedom and gives joy.

Homily at the funeral Mass for Father Giussani, February 24, 2005

Gay Marriage (2003)

Faced with the fact of homosexual unions, civil authorities adopt different positions. At times they simply tolerate the phenomenon; at other times they advocate legal recognition of such unions, under the pretext of avoiding, with regard to certain rights, discrimination against persons who live with someone of the same sex. In other cases, they favor giving homosexual unions legal equivalence to marriage properly so-called, along with the legal possibility of adopting children.

Where the government's policy is de facto tolerance and there is no explicit legal recognition of homosexual unions, it is necessary to distinguish carefully the various aspects of the problem. Moral conscience requires that, in every occasion, Christians give witness to the whole moral truth, which is contradicted both by approval of homosexual acts and unjust discrimination against homosexual persons. Therefore, discreet and prudent actions can be effective; these might involve: unmasking the way in which such tolerance might be exploited or used in the service of ideology; stating clearly the immoral nature of these unions; reminding the government of the need to contain the phenomenon within certain limits so as to safeguard public morality and, above all, to avoid exposing young people to erroneous ideas about sexuality and marriage that would deprive them of their necessary defenses and contribute to the spread of the phenomenon. Those who would move from tolerance to the legitimization of specific rights for cohabiting homosexual persons need to be reminded that the approval or legalization of evil is something far different from the toleration of evil.

In those situations where homosexual unions have been legally recognized or have been given the legal status and rights belonging to marriage, clear and emphatic opposition is a duty. One must refrain from any kind of formal cooperation in the enactment or application of such gravely unjust laws and, as far as possible, from material cooperation on the level of their application. In this area, everyone can exercise the right to conscientious objection.

Lectio magistralis on "The Spiritual Roots of Europe," Sala Capitolare, Monastery of Santa Maria sopra Minerva, Rome, May 13, 2004 (Archive of the Italian Senate)

Western Self-Hatred (2004)

The West reveals here a self-hatred that is strange and can only be considered pathological; the West is laudably trying to open itself, full of understanding, to external values, but it no longer loves itself; in its own history, it now sees only what is deplorable and destructive, while it is no longer able to perceive what is great and pure. Europe, to survive, needs a new, critical, and humble self-acceptance if it truly wishes to survive. Multiculturalism, which is so constantly and passionately encouraged and supported, sometimes amounts to an abandonment and disavowal of what is our own. But multiculturalism cannot survive without common constants, without taking one's own culture as a point of departure. It definitely can not exist without respect for what is sacred.

The movement toward the sacred elements of the other belong to this, but we can only do this if the sacred, God, is not alien to us. Of course we can and we must learn from what is sacred to others, but before others and for others it is our duty to nurture within ourselves respect for everything that is sacred and shows the face of God that appeared—the God who has compassion for the poor and the weak, widows and orphans, the foreigner; the God who is so human that he himself became man, a suffering man who by suffering together with us gave dignity and hope to pain.

Lectio magistralis on "The Spiritual Roots of Europe," Sala Capitolare, Monastery of Santa Maria sopra Minerva, Rome, May 13, 2004 (Archive of the Italian Senate)

The UN and the War on Iraq (2002)

Question: Is there a moral justification for the war?

Answer: Certainly not in this situation. There is the United Nations. It is the forum at which the final decision should be made. This should be decided by the community of peoples, not by a single power. The fact that the United Nations is looking for a way to avoid the war seems to me to provide sufficient proof that the damages would be greater than the values that would be saved . . . The UN can be criticized, but it is the instrument created after the war for a coordination of politics that is also moral.

International Days of Philosophic Thought Conference in Trieste, Italy, September 20, 2002 (*Avvenire*, September 21, 2002)

Pacifism (2005)

It's true that today a new moralism exists whose key terms are justice, peace, and conservation of creation—words that remind us of essential moral values that we truly need. But this moralism remains vague and slippery, almost inevitably so, in the sphere of party-politics. Such a moralism is above all an expectation of others, and too little a personal duty of our daily life. In fact, what does "justice" signify? Who defines it? Of what utility is peace? In recent decades we have seen amply enough in our streets and in our piazzas how pacifism can deviate toward a destructive anarchism and toward terrorism. The political moralism of the 1970s, whose roots have not yet died, was a moralism which succeeded to fascinate even those youths filled with idealism. But it was a moralism with the wrong address, inasmuch as it was deprived of serene reasoning and because, in the last analysis, it put a utopian political order above the dignity of the individual man, showing itself capable of arriving, in the name of its grand objectives, to devalue man. Political moralism, as we have seen and as we still experience, does not only fail to open the path to regeneration, but blocks it. The same is true, consequently, of a Christianity and of a theology which reduces the core of the message of Jesus, the "Kingdom of God," to "values of the Kingdom," identifying these values with the great terms of the order of political moralism, and proclaiming them, at the same time, as the synthesis of religions; thus forgetting, however, God, notwithstanding that He Himself is the proper subject and the cause of the Kingdom of God. In His place, great words (and values) remain that are capable of any type of misuse.

Conference held on April 1, 2005, at the Saint Scholastica Monastery, Subiaco

Dangers for Contemporary Man (2005)

We live in a moment of great danger and of great opportunity for man and for the world, a moment which also is one of great responsibility for all of us. During the past century, the possibilities open to man and his dominion over matter have increased to a truly unthinkable degree. His power of destruction has reached such dimensions that it at times makes one shudder. In this regard, one immediately thinks of the threat of terrorism, this new war without borders and without fronts. The fear that it can soon utilize nuclear and biologic arms is not unfounded and has brought it about that, within free States, one must have recourse to systems of security similar to those which first existed only in totalitarian states; even though there remains the feeling that all these precautions in reality cannot ever be enough, since it is neither possible nor desirable to control everything on the globe. Less visible, but no less disquieting, are the possibilities of self-manipulation which man has acquired. He has sounded out the recesses of being, deciphered the components of the human being, and now is able, or so they say, to "construct" himself by himself, so that he will no longer come into this world as a gift of the Creator, but as a product of our action—a product which therefore can also be selected according to the exigencies set by ourselves. Thus, on this man there no longer shines the splendor of his being, the image of God, which is what confers upon him his dignity and his inviolability, but only the power of human abilities. He is no longer anything but the image of man—but of what man? To this problem is added the great problems of the planet: the inequality in the distribution of the goods of the earth, the growth of poverty, indeed of impoverishment, the exploitation of the earth and of its resources, famine, sicknesses that threaten the entire world, the conflict of cultures. All this shows that the growth of the possibilities open to us does not correspond to an equivalent growth in our moral energy. The moral force has not grown together with the development of science. Indeed, it has rather diminished, because the mentality of technology confines morality in the subjective sphere, while we have need in fact of a public morality—a morality which knows how to respond to the threats which weigh down the existence of us all. The true, most grave danger of the present moment is found precisely in this disequilibrium between technological possibilities and moral energy. The security, of which we have need as a presupposition of our liberty and of our dignity, cannot in the last analysis come about in technological systems of control, but, in a word, can arise only from the moral force of man. Where this is lacking or is insufficient, the power which man has will always be transformed more and more into a power for destruction.

Conference held on April 1, 2005, at the Saint Scholastica Monastery, Subiaco

Power (2005)

Jesus, condemned as an imposter king, is mocked, but this very mockery lays bare a painful truth. How often are the symbols of power, borne by the great ones of this world, an affront to truth, to justice, and to the dignity of man! How many times is their pomp and their lofty words nothing but grandiose lies, a parody of their solemn obligation to serve the common good! It is because Jesus is mocked and wears the crown of suffering that he appears as the true King. His scepter is justice (cf. Ps 45:7). The price of justice in this world is suffering: Jesus, the true King, does not reign through violence, but through a love which suffers for us and with us. He takes up the Cross, our cross, the burden of being human, the burden of the world. And so he goes before us and points out to us the way which leads to true life.

Meditations for the Way of the Cross 2005, at the Coliseum in Rome on March 25, 2005 (Vatican Information Service)

Relativism (2005)

How many winds of doctrine have we known in recent decades, how many ideological currents, how many ways of thinking? The small boat of the thought of many Christians has often been tossed about by these waves—flung from one extreme to another: from Marxism to liberalism, even to libertinism; from collectivism to radical individualism; from atheism to a vague religious mysticism; from agnosticism to syncretism and so forth. Every day new sects spring up, and what Saint Paul says about human deception and the trickery that strives to entice people into error (cf. Eph 4:14) comes true.

Today, having a clear faith based on the Creed of the Church is often labeled as fundamentalism. Whereas relativism, that is, letting oneself be "tossed here and there, carried about by every wind of doctrine," seems the only attitude that can cope with modern times. We are building a dictatorship of relativism that does not recognize anything as definitive and whose ultimate goal consists solely of one's own ego and desires.

Mass *Pro eligendo Romano Pontifice*, homily by Cardinal Ratzinger, Vatican City, April 18, 2005 (*L'Osservatore Romano*)

Scientific Research and Human Dignity (2004)

The first element is the "unconditionality" with which human dignity and human rights must be presented as values that precede any jurisdiction on the part of the state. These basic rights are not created by the legislator, nor conferred on the citizens, "but rather exist in their own right, are always to be respected by the legislator, are given previously to him as values of a superior order." This validity of human dignity, previous to every political action and to every political decision, refers back ultimately to the Creator: only He can establish values that are founded on the essence of man and that are intangible. That there be values that cannot be manipulated by anyone is the real, true guarantee of our freedom and of man's greatness; Christian faith sees in this the mystery of the Creator and of the condition of the image of God that He conferred upon man. Now, almost no one these days would directly deny the precedence of human dignity and basic human rights over all political decisions; the horrors of Nazism and its racist theories are still too recent. But in the concrete sphere of the so-called progress of medicine there are very real threats to these values: whether we think of cloning, or of the conservation of human fetuses for organ donation, or of the whole field of genetic manipulation—no one can ignore the gradual erosion of human dignity that threatens us here.

Conference held on April 1, 2005, at the Saint Scholastica Monastery, Subiaco

Science and Technology (1987)

Science and technology are valuable resources for man when placed at his service and when they promote his integral development for the benefit of all; but they cannot of themselves show the meaning of existence and of human progress. Being ordered to man, who initiates and develops them, they draw from the person and his moral values the indication of their purpose and the awareness of their limits.

It would on the one hand be illusory to claim that scientific research and its applications are morally neutral; on the other hand one cannot derive criteria for guidance from mere technical efficiency, from research's possible usefulness to some at the expense of others, or, worse still, from prevailing ideologies. Thus science and technology require, for their own intrinsic meaning, an unconditional respect for the fundamental criteria of the moral law: that is to say, they must be at the service of the human person, of his inalienable rights and his true and integral good according to the design and will of God. The rapid development of technological discoveries gives greater urgency to this need to respect the criteria just mentioned: science without conscience can only lead to man's ruin.

Donum Vitae, instruction on respect for human life in its origin and on the dignity of procreation, Vatican City, February 22, 1987 (Vatican Information Service)

Does the Holy Spirit Choose the Pope
in the Conclave? (1997)

I would not say so, in the sense that the Holy Spirit picks out the pope . . . I would say that the Spirit does not exactly take control of the affair, but rather like a good educator, as it were, leaves us much space, much freedom, without entirely abandoning us. Thus the Spirit's role should be understood in a much more elastic sense, not that he dictates the candidate for whom one must vote. Probably the only assurance he offers is that the thing cannot be totally ruined.

Bavaria TV, interview with Cardinal Ratzinger (from the *National Catholic Reporter*, April 15, 2005)

From the First Message of His Holiness Benedict XVI
at the End of the Eucharistic Concelebration with the
Members of the College of Cardinals in the Sistine Chapel

Wednesday, April 20, 2005

In my soul there are two contrasting sentiments in these hours. On the one hand, a sense of inadequacy and human turmoil for the responsibility entrusted to me yesterday as the Successor of the Apostle Peter in this See of Rome, with regard to the Universal Church. On the other hand I sense within me profound gratitude to God Who—as the liturgy makes us sing—does not abandon His flock, but leads it throughout time, under the guidance of those whom He has chosen as vicars of His Son, and made pastors. This intimate recognition for a gift of divine mercy prevails in my heart in spite of everything. I consider this a grace obtained for me by my venerated predecessor, John Paul II. It seems I can feel his strong hand squeezing mine; I seem to see his smiling eyes and listen to his words, addressed to me especially at this moment: "Do not be afraid!"

The death of the Holy Father John Paul II, and the days which followed, were for the Church and for the entire world an extraordinary time of grace. The great pain for his death and the void that it left in all of us were tempered by the action of the Risen Christ, which showed itself during long days in the choral wave of faith, love, and spiritual solidarity, culminating in his solemn funeral. We can say it: the funeral of John Paul II was a truly extraordinary experience in which was perceived in some way the power of God Who, through His Church, wishes to form a great family of all peoples, through the unifying force of Truth and Love. In the hour of death, conformed to his Master and Lord, John Paul II crowned his long and fruitful pontificate, confirming the Christian people in faith, gathering them around him and making the entire human family feel more united. How can one not feel sustained by this witness? How can one not feel the encouragement that comes from this event of grace?

Surprising every prevision I had, Divine Providence, through the will of the venerable Cardinal Fathers, called me to succeed this great Pope. I have been thinking in these hours about what happened in the region of Cesarea of Phillippi two thousand years ago: I seem to hear the words of Peter: "You are Christ, the Son of the living God," and the solemn affirmation of the Lord: "You are Peter and on this rock I will build my Church . . . I will give you the keys of the kingdom of heaven."

You are Christ! You are Peter! It seems I am reliving this very Gospel scene; I, the Successor of Peter, repeat with trepidation the anxious words of the fisherman from Galilee and I listen again with intimate emotion to the reassuring promise of the divine Master. If the weight of the responsibility that now lies on my poor shoulders is enormous, the divine power on which I can count is surely immeasurable: "You are Peter and on this rock I will build my Church." Electing me as the Bishop of Rome, the Lord wanted me as his Vicar, he wished me to be the "rock" upon which everyone may rest with confidence. I ask him to make up for the poverty of my strength, that I may be a courageous and faithful pastor of His flock, always docile to the inspirations of His Spirit. (…)

Before my eyes is, in particular, the witness of Pope John Paul II. He leaves us a Church that is more courageous, freer, younger. A Church that, according to his teaching and example, looks with serenity to the past and is not afraid of the future. With the Great Jubilee the Church was introduced into the new millennium carrying in her hands the Gospel, applied to the world through the authoritative rereading of Vatican Council II. (…)

In this moment, I go back in my memory to the unforgettable experience we all underwent with the death and the funeral of the lamented John Paul II. Around his mortal remains, lying on the bare earth, leaders of nations gathered, with people from all social classes and especially the young, in an unforgettable embrace of affection and admiration. The entire world looked to him with trust. To many it seemed as if that intense participation, amplified to the confines of the planet by the social communications media, was like a choral request for help addressed to the Pope by modern humanity which, wracked by fear and uncertainty, questions itself about the future.

The Church today must revive within herself an awareness of the task to present the world again with the voice of the One Who said: "I am the light of the world; he who follows me will not walk in darkness but will have the light of life." In undertaking his ministry, the new Pope knows that his task is to bring the light of Christ to shine before the men and women of today: not his own light but that of Christ.

With this awareness, I address myself to everyone, even to those who follow other religions or who are simply seeking an answer to the fundamental questions of life and have not yet found it. I address everyone with simplicity and affection, to assure them that the Church wants to continue to build an open and sincere dialogue with them, in a search for the true good of mankind and of society.

From God I invoke unity and peace for the human family and declare the willingness of all Catholics to cooperate for true social development, one that respects the dignity of all human beings.

I will make every effort and dedicate myself to pursuing the promising dialogue that my predecessors began with various civilizations, because it is mutual understanding that gives rise to conditions for a better future for everyone.

NOTES

1. ROMAN SPRING

1. "In depth report: Pope John Paul II," BBC News, April 2005.
2. John Paul II, Christmas message, Vatican City, December 25, 1990.
3. "In depth report: Pope John Paul II," BBC News, April 2005.
4. Associated Press, April 15, 2005.
5. Associated Press, April 15, 2005.
6. "Joseph Ratzinger, Mess. Pro Eligendo Romano Pontefice," *Vatican Basilica,* April 18, 2005.

2. BAVARIA

1. Joseph Ratzinger, *Milestones: Memoirs (1927–1977)*, San Francisco: Ignatius Press, 1998, p. 8.
2. John Allen, *Cardinal Ratzinger: The Vatican's Enforcer of the Faith*, New York: Continuum International Publishing Group, 2001.
3. Associated Press, April 19, 2005.
4. ANSA Italian News Agency, April 19, 2005.
5. Massimo L. Salvadori, *Storia dell'età contemporanea*, 1985.
6. *Corriere della Sera,* April 20, 2005.
7. Massimo L. Salvadori, *Storia dell'età contemporanea*, 1985.
8. *La Repubblica,* April 21, 2005; *New York Times,* April 22, 2005.
9. Joseph Ratzinger, *Milestones: Memoirs (1927–1977)*, San Francisco: Ignatius Press, 1998.
10. *Corriere della Sera,* April 21, 2005.
11. John Paul II, biographical notes, *L'Osservatore Romano,* www.vatican.va.
12. Joseph Ratzinger, *Milestones*; John Allen, *Cardinal Ratzinger; The Telegraph,* April 21, 2005; *New York Times,* April 21, 2005; *Corriere della Sera,* April 20, 2005; ANSA, April 20, 2005.

3. FROM THE HORRORS TO THE ALTAR

1. *Corriere della Sera*, April 21, 2005.
2. Joseph Ratzinger, *Milestones*.
3. Ibid.
4. Joseph Ratzinger, *Milestones*; John Allen, *Cardinal Ratzinger*.
5. *Associated Press*, April 19, 2005.
6. ANSA, April 22, 2005.
7. Benedict XVI, biographical notes, *L'Osservatore Romano*, www.vatican.va.
8. Ibid.
9. Ibid.

4. MUSIC AND BEAUTY

1. Joseph Ratzinger, "La corrispondenza del cuore nell'incontro con la bellezza," 30 Giorni, August 2002.
2. Joseph Ratzinger with Peter Seewald, *Salt of the Earth: The Church at the End of the Millennium*, San Francisco: Ignatius Press, 1997, p.47.
3. David L. Schindler, *Hans Urs von Balthasar: His Life and Work*, San Francisco: Ignatius Press, 1991.
4. Hans Urs von Balthasar, *The Glory of the Lord: A Theological Aesthetics*, Edinburgh: T&T Clark, 1982.
5. David L. Schindler, *Hans Urs von Balthasar*.

5. THE COUNCIL YEARS

1. "The Tablet," *International Catholic Newspaper*, April 19, 1997.
2. *Die Stadt*, Bonn, April 20, 2005, www.bonn.de/familie_gesellschaft_bildung_soziales/topthemen/02331/?lang=de.
3. Author interview with Monsignor Lorenzo Albacete, April 21, 2005.
4. ANSA Italian news agency, April 19, 2005.
5. ANSA, April 22, 2005.
6. *L'Osservatore Romano*, September 6, 2000, www.vatican.va.
7. *Avvenire*, April 19, 2005; New York Times, April 22, 2005.
8. *Corriere della Sera*, April 21, 2005.
9. *Corriere della Sera*, April 21, 2005.

6. NINETEEN SIXTY-EIGHT

1. Eberhard-Karls University official website, www.uni-tuebingen.de.
2. *La Repubblica*, October 4, 1985.
3. ANSA, April 19, 2005.
4. Joseph Ratzinger with Peter Seewald, *Salt of the Earth: The Church at the*

End of the Millennium, San Francisco: Ignatius Press, 1997.
5. Seminar of the Pontifical Council for the Laity, Vatican City, June 17, 1999.
6. Ibid.
7. Joseph Ratzinger, *Un Avvenimento di vita, cioè una Storia* (Introduction), Rome: Il Sabato, 1993.

7. HANS, HENRI, AND JOSEPH

1. *Avvenire*, April 19, 2005.
2. Andrea Schulte-Peevers, *Bavaria*, Lonely Planet Publication, 2002.
3. *New York Times*, April 22, 2005.
4. *New York Times*, April 22, 2005.
5. Lecture by H. E. Cardinal Ratzinger, "Eucharist, communion and solidariety," given at the Bishops' Conference of the region of Campania in Benevento (Italy), June 2, 2002.
6. Joseph Ratzinger, *Communio: A Program*, in *Communio—International Catholic Review*, Washington, D.C., Fall 2002.
7. Ibid.
8. Ibid.
9. Ibid.
10. Message from John Paul II, *Communio*, from the review website, www.communio-icr.com.
11. Author interview with David L. Schindler, New York, April 20, 2005.

8. THE ARCHBISHOP

1. Hans Urs von Balthasar and Joseph Ratzinger, *Perché sono ancora cristiano—Perché sono ancora nella chiesa*, Rome: Queriniana, 1976.
2. Joseph Ratzinger and Vittorio Messori, *The Ratzinger Report*, San Francisco: Ignatius, 1985.
3. *30 Days*, August 2003.
4. Ibid.
5. Ibid.

9. FROM MUNICH TO ROME

1. Address of Cardinal Joseph Ratzinger at the beginning of the thanksgiving Mass for the twenty-fifth anniversary of the pontificate of John Paul II, Vatican City, October 16, 2003.
2. Interview with Wienfried Röhmel, *Avvenire*, April 22, 2005.

10. THE FIRST YEARS IN ROME

1. *L'Osservatore Romano*, April 2005, www.vatican.va.

2. ANSA, March 30, 1982.

3. John Paul II, meeting with members of the media, Vatican City, ANSA, January 27, 1984.

4. Cardinal Joseph Ratzinger, homily at Mass for members of the media, Vatican City, ANSA, January 27, 1984.

5. *Corriere della Sera*, April 20, 2005.

11. THE DISPUTES

1. *Morto monsignor Lefebvre*, March 25, 1991.

2. Ibid.

3. *Avvenire*, April 19, 2005.

4. Ibid.

5. Congregation for the Doctrine of the Faith, Instruction on certain aspects of the "Theology of Liberation"—Libertatis nuntius, Vatican City, August 6, 1984 (Libreria Editrice Vaticana).

6. John Paul II, *Sollecitudo rei socialis*, Vatican City, December 30, 1987 (Libreria Editrice Vaticana).

7. ANSA, September 5, 1984.

8. Congregation for the Doctrine of the Faith, Instruction on certain aspects of the "Theology of Liberation"—Libertatis nuntius, Vatican City, August 6, 1984 (Libreria Editrice Vaticana).

9. *Avvenire*, April 19, 2005.

10. BBC News, "Pope Benedict XVI: In depth," April 20, 2005.

11. ANSA, April 19, 2005.

12. *New York Times*, April 23, 2005.

13. Congregation for the Doctrine of the Faith, Declaration regarding certain aspects of the theological doctrine of Professor Hans Küng—Christi ecclesia, Vatican City, December 15, 1979 (Libreria Editrice Vaticana).

14. Congregation for the Doctrine of the Faith, Declaration regarding the dialogues with Rev. Fr. Edward Schillebeeckx on certain aspects of his doctrinal christology, Vatican City, December 13, 1979 (Libreria Editrice Vaticana).

15. Congregation for the Doctrine of the Faith, Letter to Father Edward Schillebeeckx regarding his book *Kerkelijk Ambt* (*The ministry in the Church*, 1980), Vatican City, August 6, 1984 (Libreria Editrice Vaticana).

16. *New York Times*, April 24, 2005.

17. *New York Times*, June 25, 1984.

18. Congregation for the Doctrine of the Faith, Notification on the book *Mary and Human Liberation* of Fr. Tissa Balasuriya, O.M.I., Vatican City, January 2, 1997 (Libreria Editrice Vaticana).

19. Congregation for the Doctrine of the Faith, Letter regarding the suspension of Carlo Curran from the teaching of theology, Vatican City, July 25, 1986 (Libreria Editrice Vaticana).

20. ANSA, April 16, 1997.

12. DOMINUS JESUS

1. Congregation for the Doctrine of the Faith, *Declaration on Masonic Associations*, Vatican City, November 26, 1983 (Libreria Editrice Vaticana).

2. *Lectio magistralis* on "Le radici spirituali dell'Europa," Sala Capitolare, Monastery of Saint Maria sopra Minerva, Rome, May 13, 2004 (archive of the Senate of the Republic).

3. Conference, *Mental Handicaps Today*, Vatican City, November 28, 1996 (ANSA).

4. Ibid.

5. John Paul II, "*Veritatis Splendor*," Vatican City, August 6, 1993 (Libreria Editrice Vaticana).

6. ANSA, October 3, 1993.

7. *Catechism of the Catholic Church*, Vatican City, 1992 (Libreria Editrice Vaticana).

8. Joseph Ratzinger, "*Current Doctrinal Relevance of the Catechism of the Catholic Church*," Vatican City, October 9, 1992 (Libreria Editrice Vaticana).

9. Ibid.

10. John Paul II, "*Evangelium Vitae*," Vatican City, March 25, 1995 (Libreria Editrice Vaticana).

11. Congregation for the Doctrine of the Faith, *Declaration on the unity and salvific universality of Jesus Christ and the Church—Dominus Jesus*, Vatican City, August 6, 2000 (Libreria Editrice Vaticana).

12. Ibid.

13. Ibid.

14. Joseph Ratzinger, press conference for the presentation of the Declaration *Dominus Jesus*, Vatican City, September 5, 2000 (Libreria Editrice Vaticana).

15. Ibid.

16. Ibid.

17. ANSA, September 7, 2000.

18. ANSA, September 8, 2000.

19. ANSA, September 25, 2000.

20. ANSA, October 1, 2000.

21. Ibid.

13. A NEW POPE

1. Office of the liturgical celebration of the Supreme Pontiff, Way of the Cross, March 25, 2005 (Libreria Editrice Vaticana).

2. Ibid.

3. Ibid.

4. Ibid.

5. Ibid.

6. Homily of Cardinal Joseph Ratzinger for the funeral mass of Mons. Luigi Giussani, Milan, February 24, 2005 (Libreria Editrice Vaticana).

7. Homily for the Easter Vigil mass, Vatican City, March 26, 2005 (Libreria Editrice Vaticana).

8. Joseph Ratzinger, L'Europa nella crisi delle culture Conference, Subiaco, Italy, April 1, 2005 (Libreria Editrice Vaticana).

9. Funeral mass of the Roman pontiff John Paul II, Homily of His Eminence Cardinal Joseph Ratzinger, Vatican City, April 8, 2005 (Libreria Editrice Vaticana).

10. President speaks to press pool, aboard Air Force One en route to Waco, Texas, April 8, 2005 (Office of the press secretary, White House).

11. Mass Pro eligendo Romano pontefice, Homily of His Eminence Cardinal Joseph Ratzinger, Vatican City, April 18, 2005.

12. Joseph Ratzinger, Saint Peter's Square, Vatican City, April 19, 2005 (Libreria Editrice Vaticana).

13. ANSA, Vatican City, April 25, 2005.

14. Mass for the inauguration of the pontificate of Benedict XVI, Homily of the Holy Father, Vatican City, April 24, 2005 (Libreria Editrice Vaticana).